extreme
waiting for the punchline

Editor: Jeannette DeLisa
Transcribed by Carl Culpepper and Hemme Lüttjeboer
Transcrition Editor: Colgan Bryan
Book Design: Joseph Klucar
Photography: Michael Halsband

© 1995 WARNER BROS. PUBLICATIONS INC.
All Rights Reserved

Any duplication, adaptation or arrangement of the compositions
contained in this collection requires the written consent of the Publisher.
No part of this book may be photocopied or reproduced in any way without permission.
Unauthorized uses are an infringement of U.S. Copyright Act and are punishable by Law.

contents

cynical 16

evilangelist 38

hip today 5

leave me alone 50

midnight express 59

naked 68

no respect 81

shadow boxing 90

tell me something i don't know . . .103

there is no god 114

unconditionally 28

waiting for the punchline 125

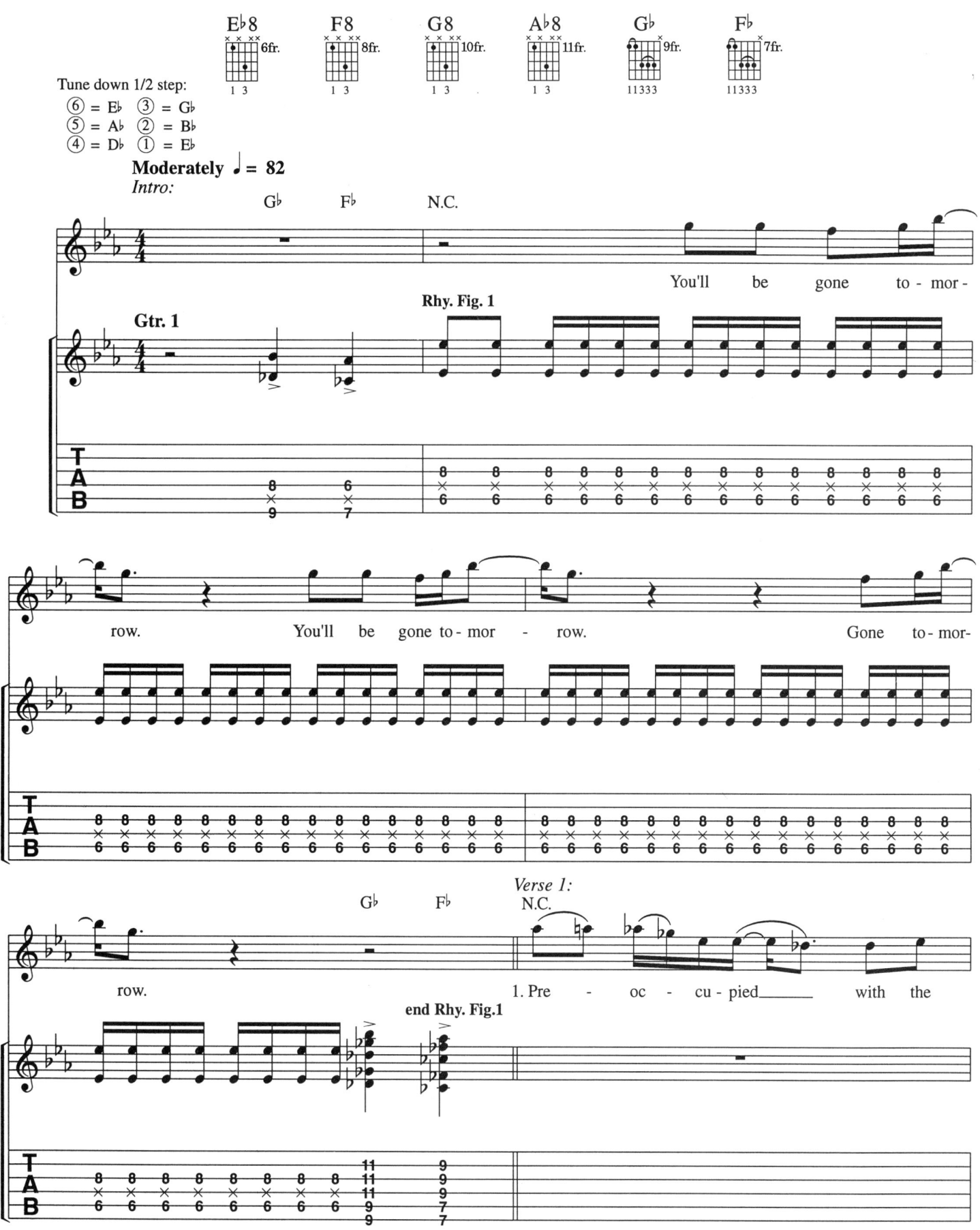

6

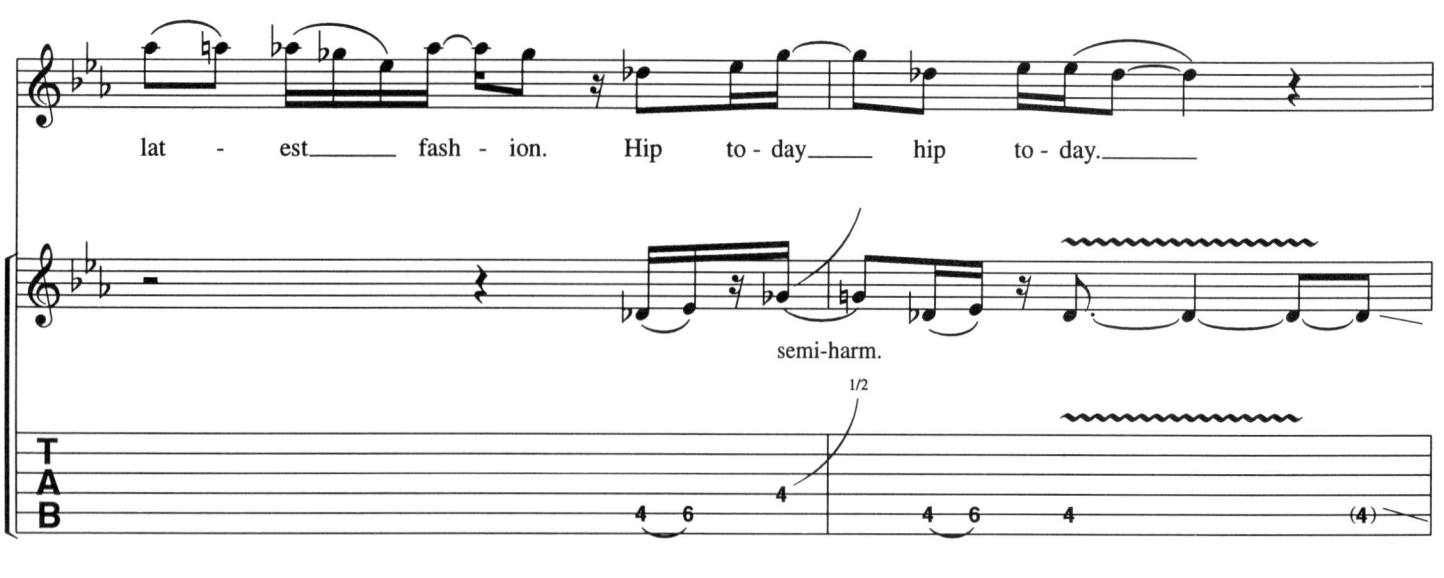

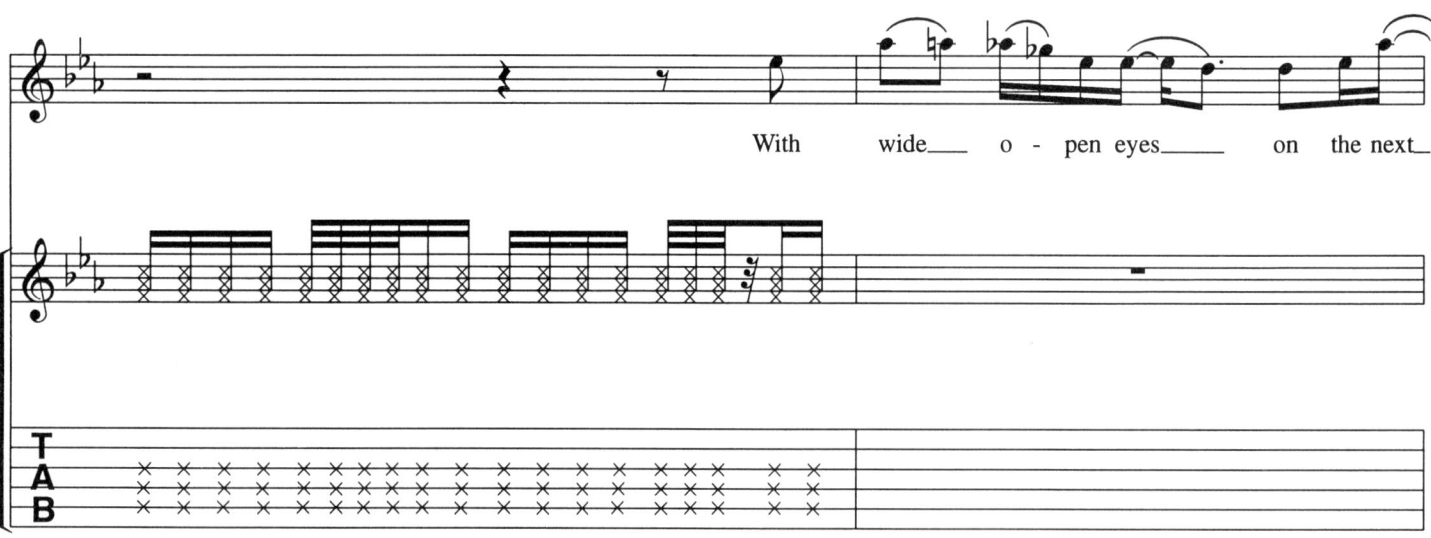

Hip Today - 11 - 2
PG9515

9

Hip Today - 11 - 5
PG9515

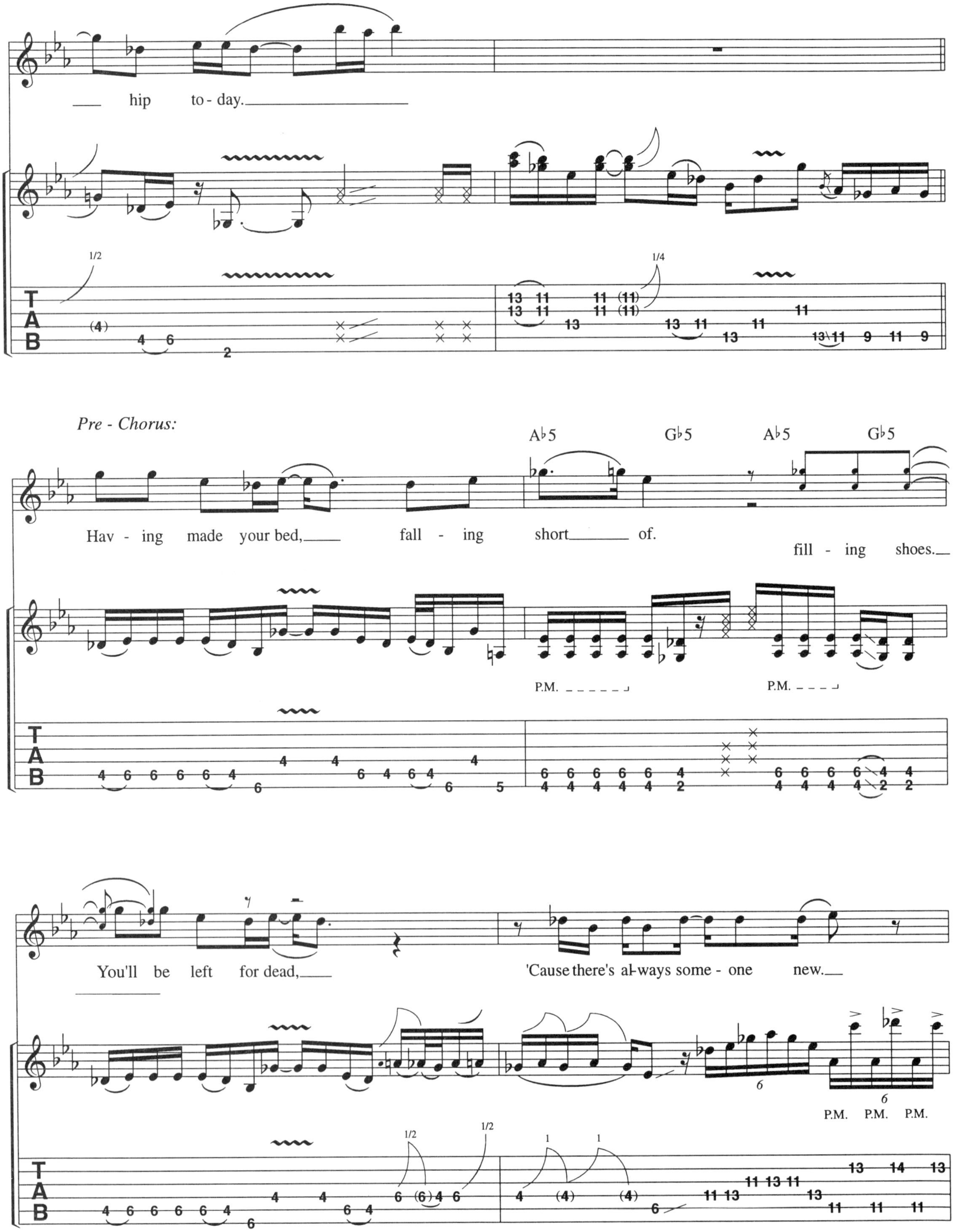
hip to - day.
Pre - Chorus:
Ab5
Gb5
Ab5
Gb5
Hav - ing made your bed, fall - ing short of.
fill - ing shoes.
P.M.
P.M.
You'll be left for dead,
'Cause there's al-ways some - one new.
P.M. P.M. P.M.
TAB

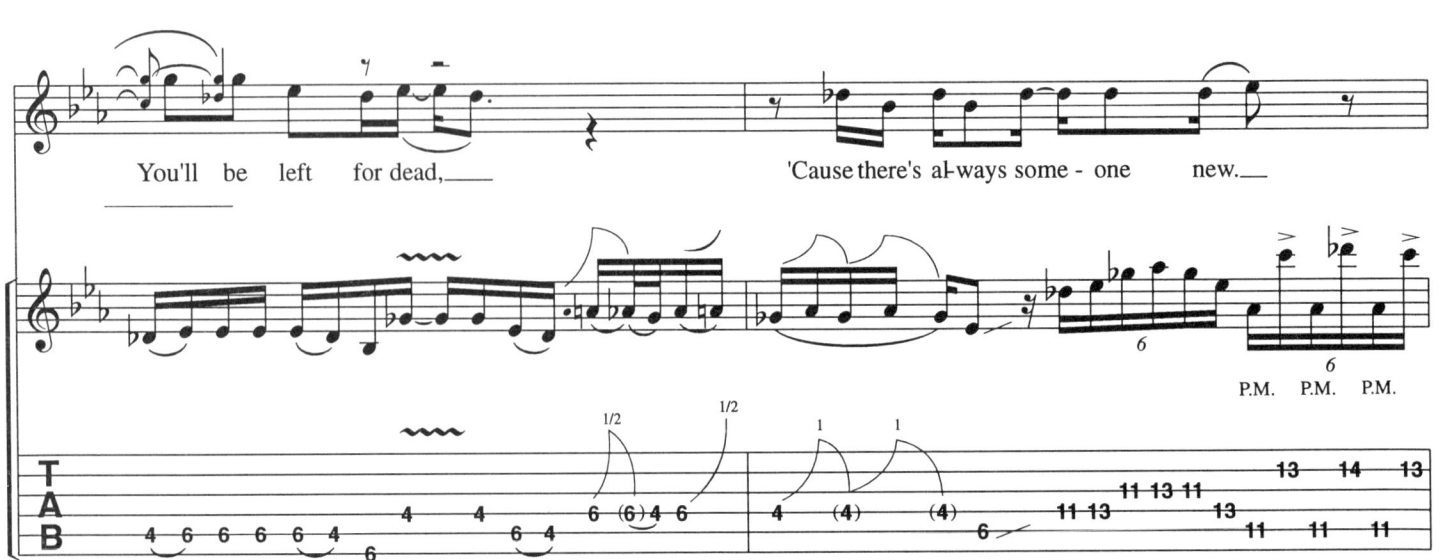

12

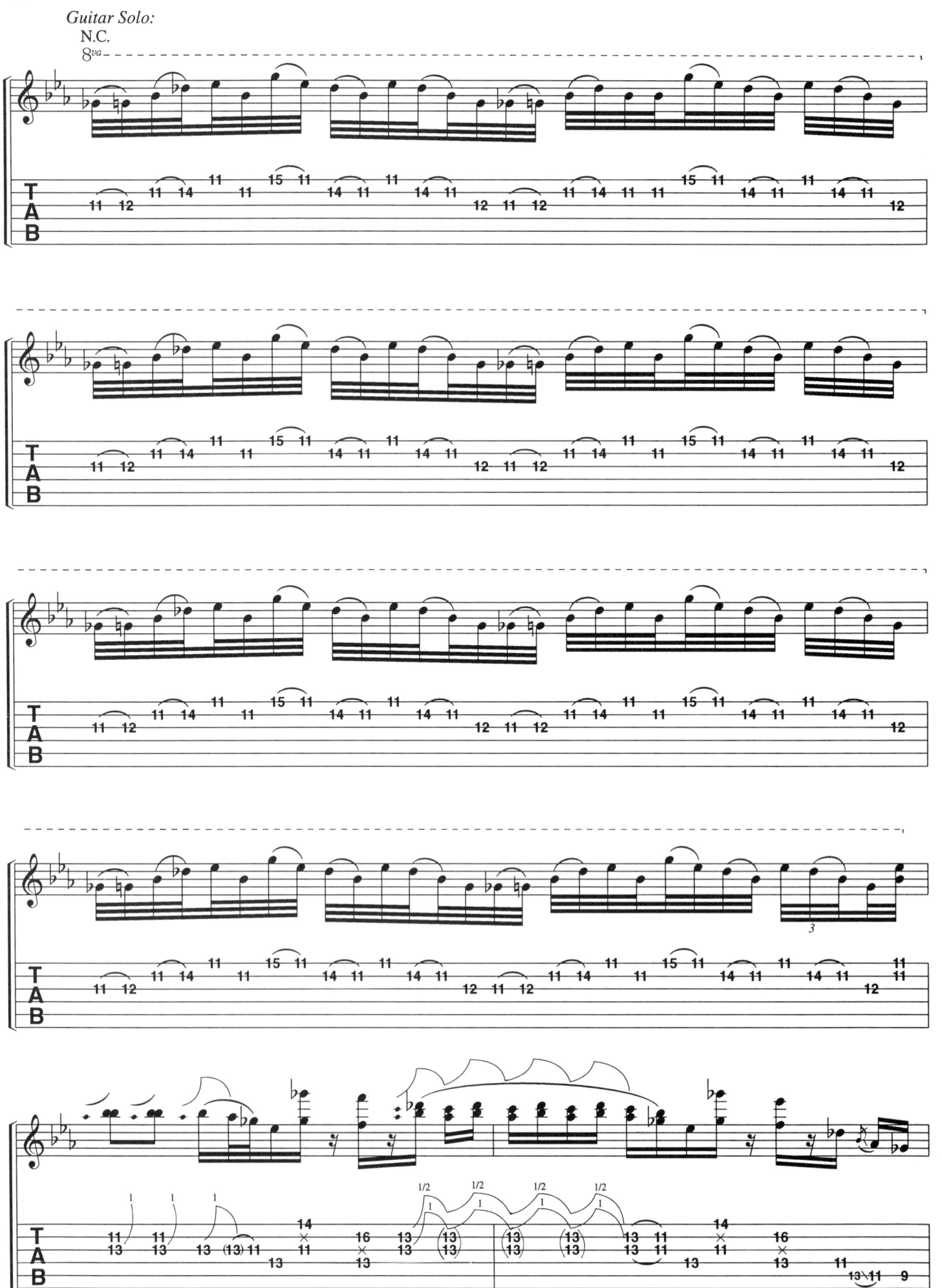

Hip Today - 11 - 8
PG9515

13

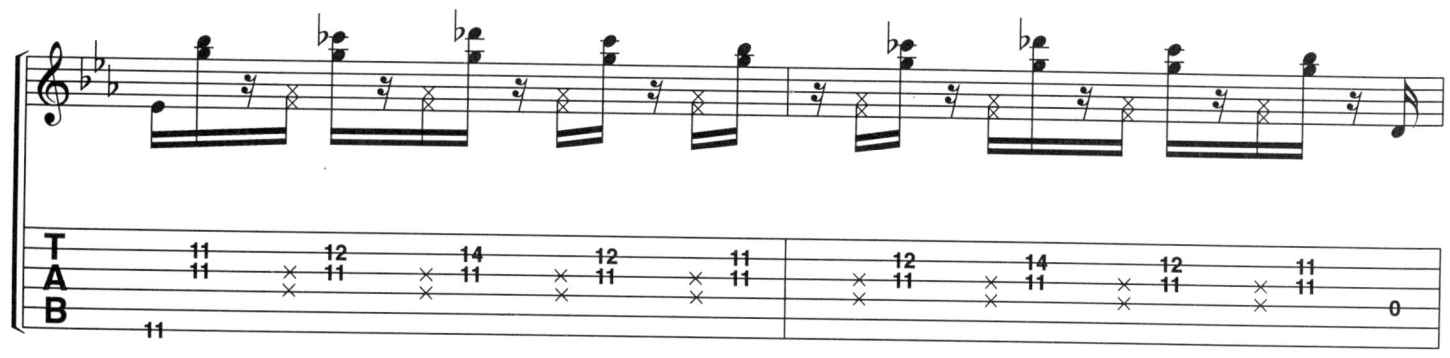

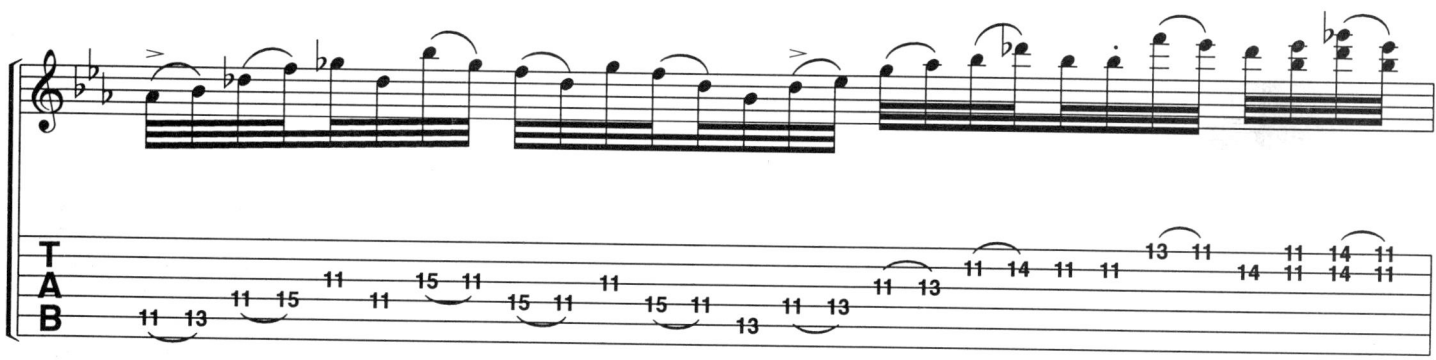

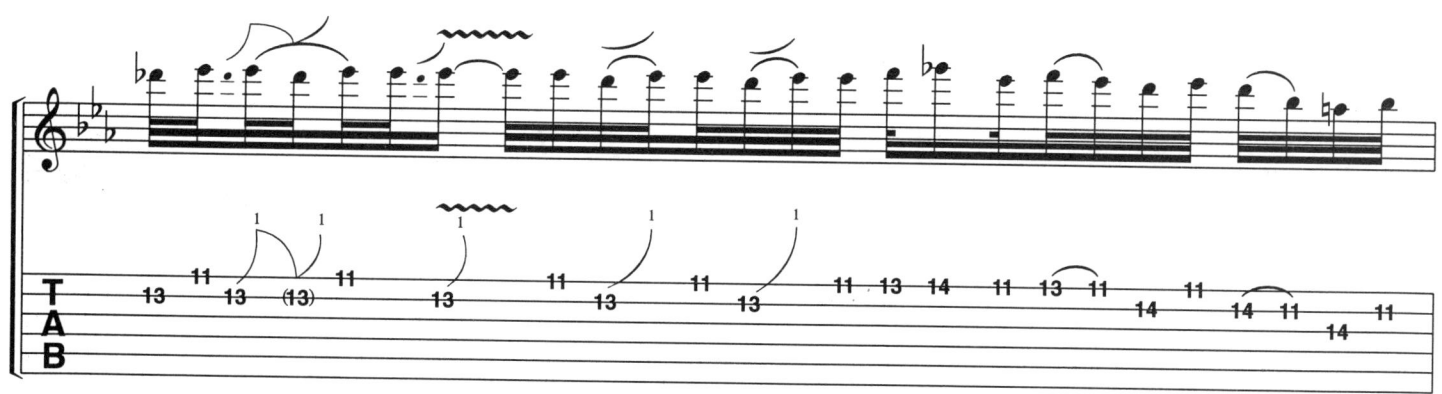

Hip Today - 11 - 9
PG9515

14

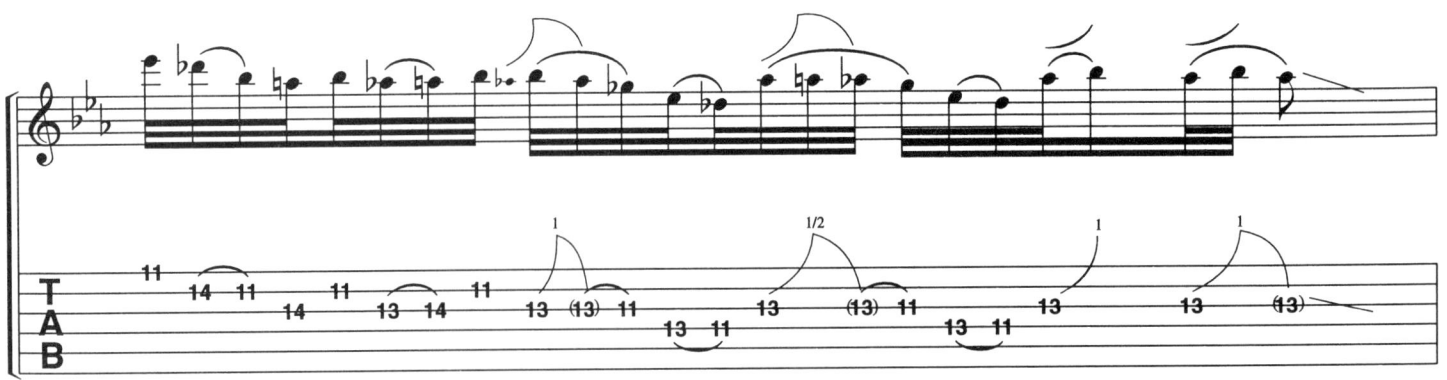

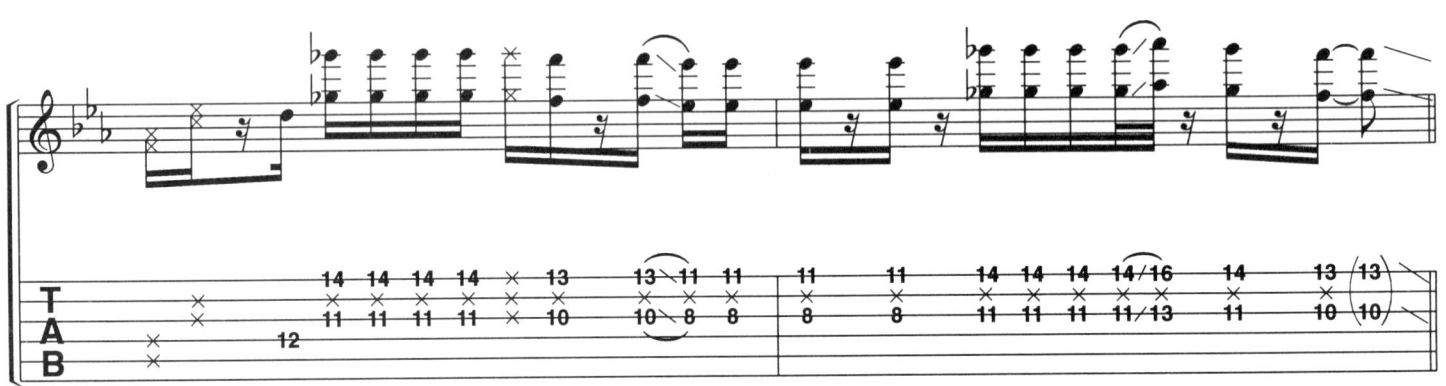

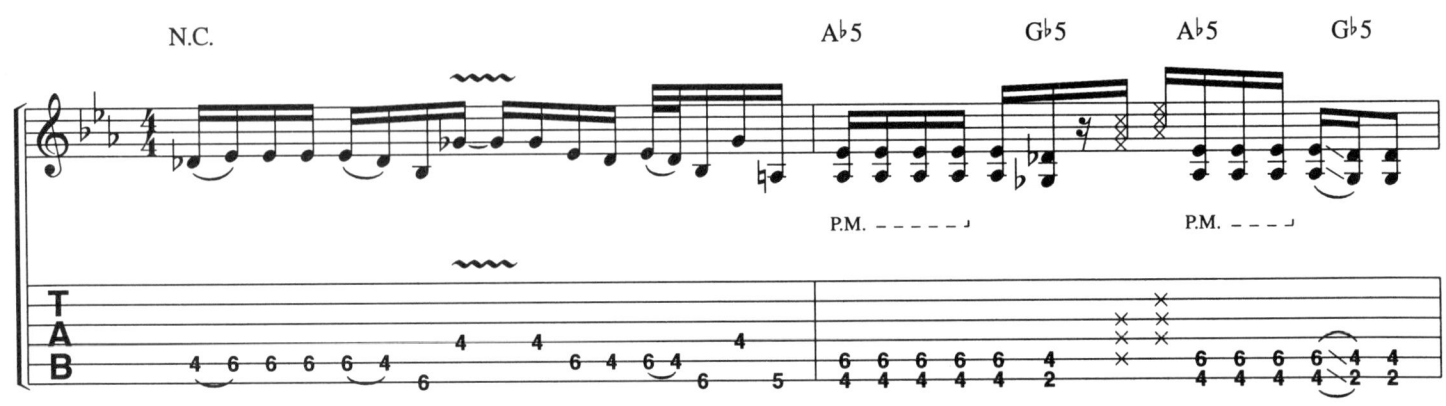

Hip Today - 11 - 10
PG9515

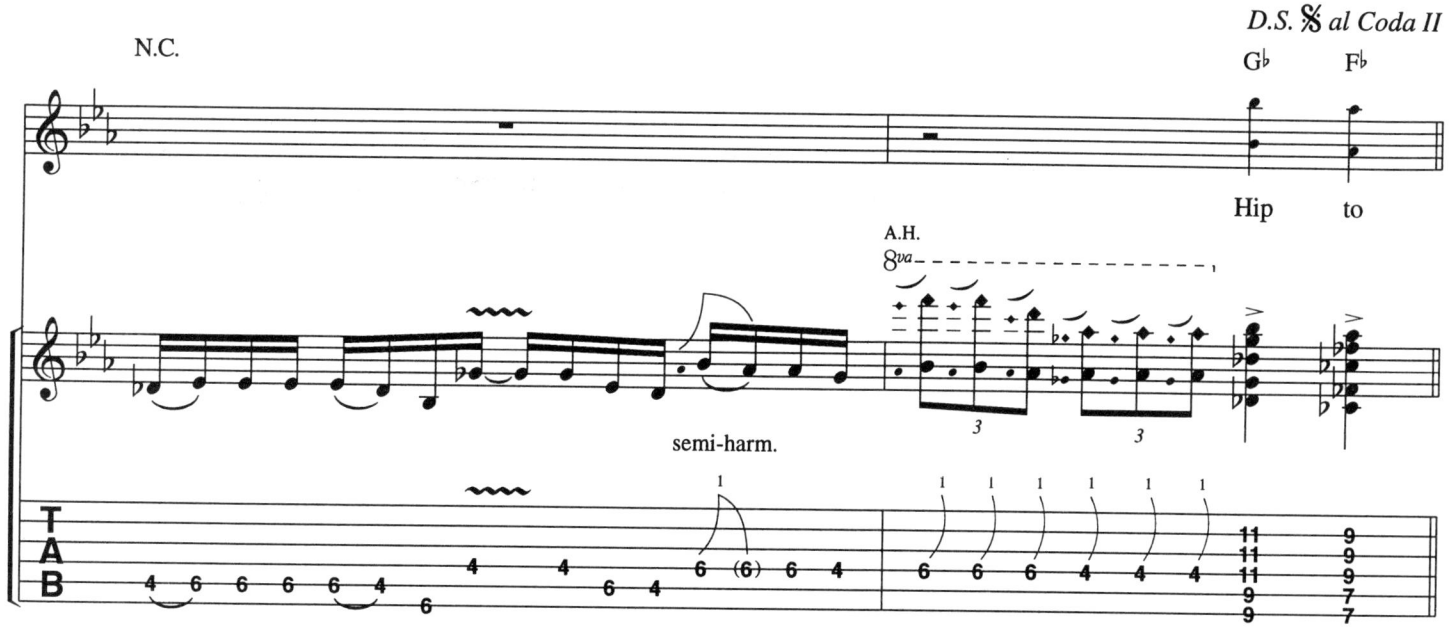

cynical

Words and Music by
NUNO BETTENCOURT/GARY CHERONE

All gtrs. tuned:
⑥ = D♭   ③ = G♭
⑤ = A♭   ② = B♭
④ = D♭   ① = E♭

Moderately ♩ = 100

Intro:

Verse 1 & 2:

1. To - day   don't   look   so
2. And   what - ev - er   you

Cynical - 12 - 1
PG9515

Copyright © 1995 COLOR ME BLIND MUSIC (ASCAP)
All Rights Administered by ALMO MUSIC CORP. Throughout the World Under License from FUNKY METAL MUSIC, INC.
International Copyright Secured   Made in U.S.A.   All Rights Reserved

bad
do,
com - pared to to - mor - row.
some-one's done it first.
If time is all we
Though it's sad but true,
have,
then we're liv - ing on bor - rowed.
ah, this is just an - oth - er verse.
TAB
TAB
TAB

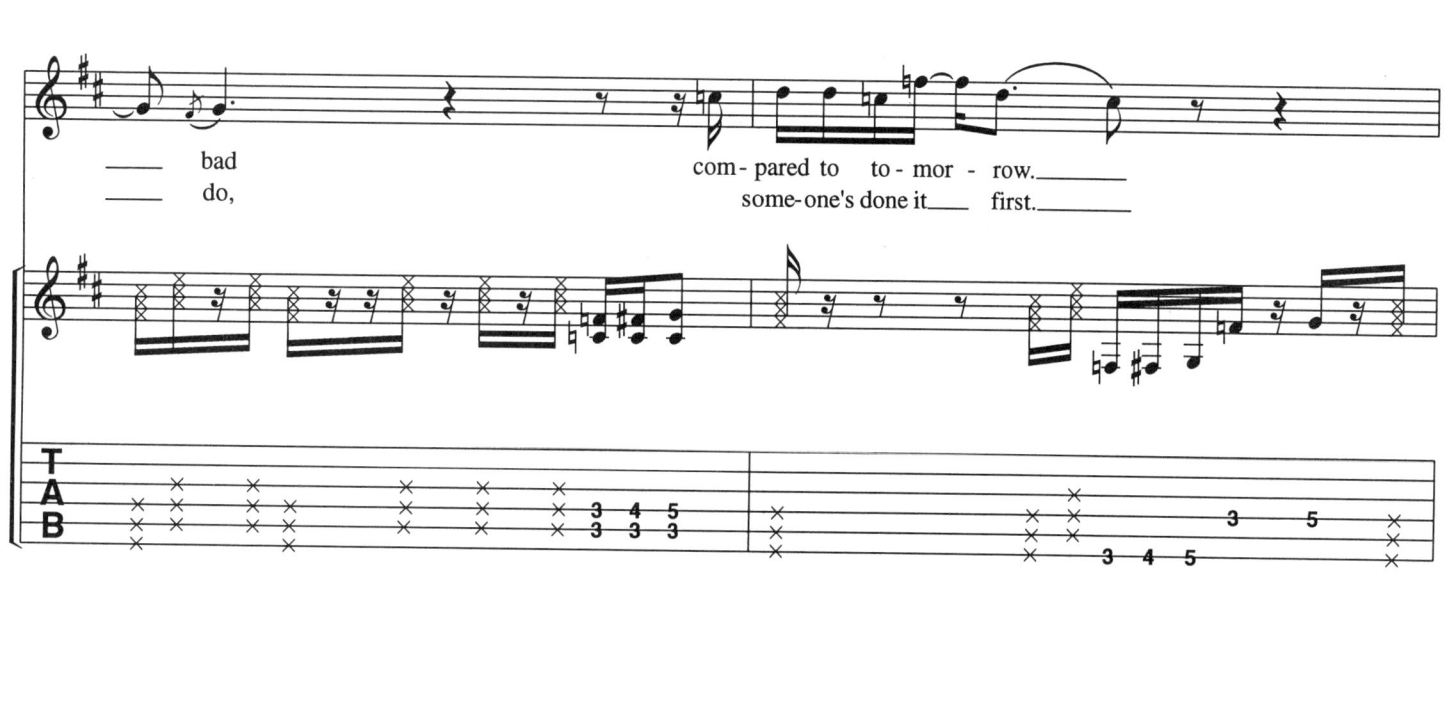

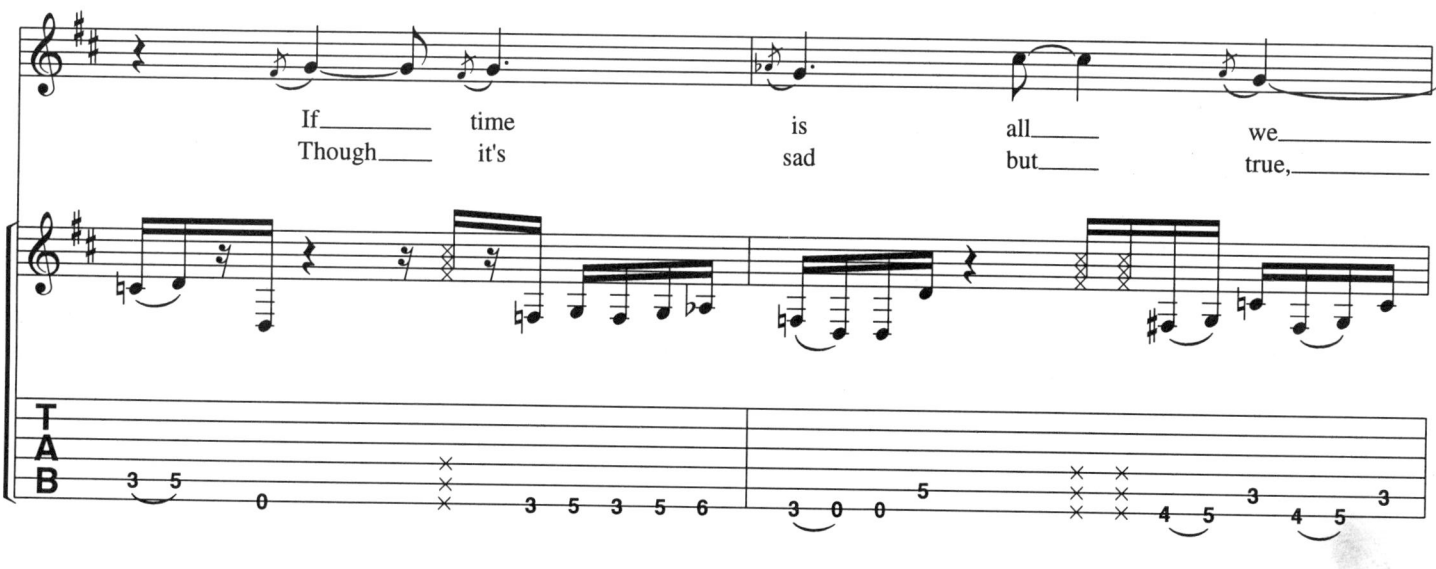

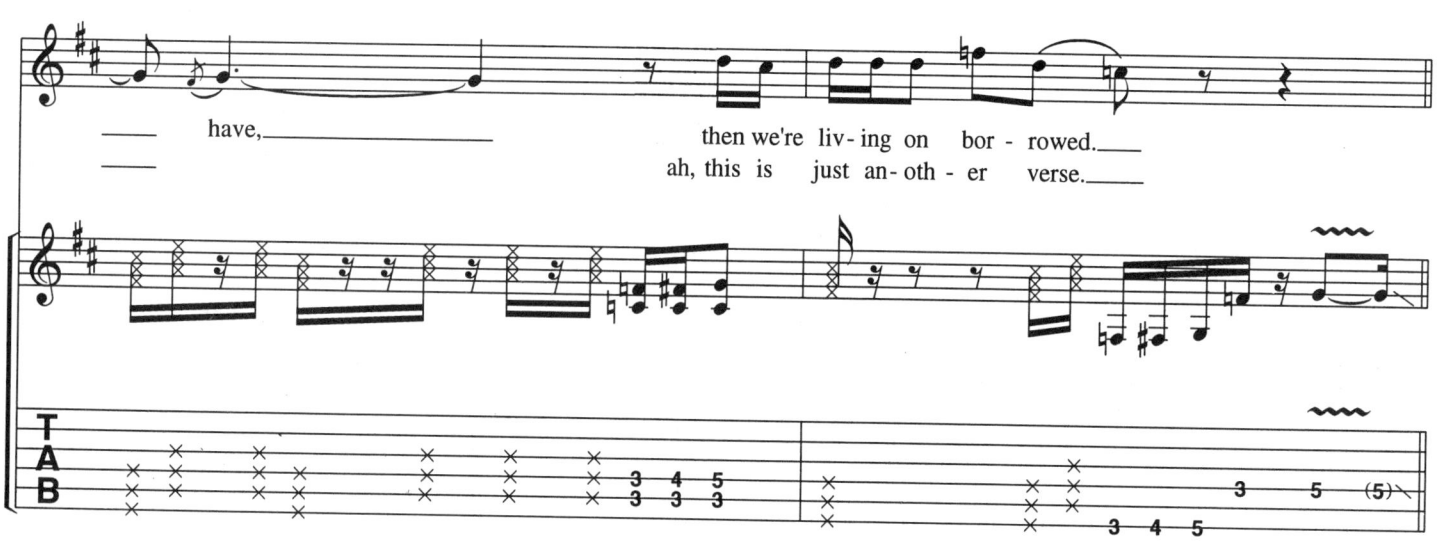

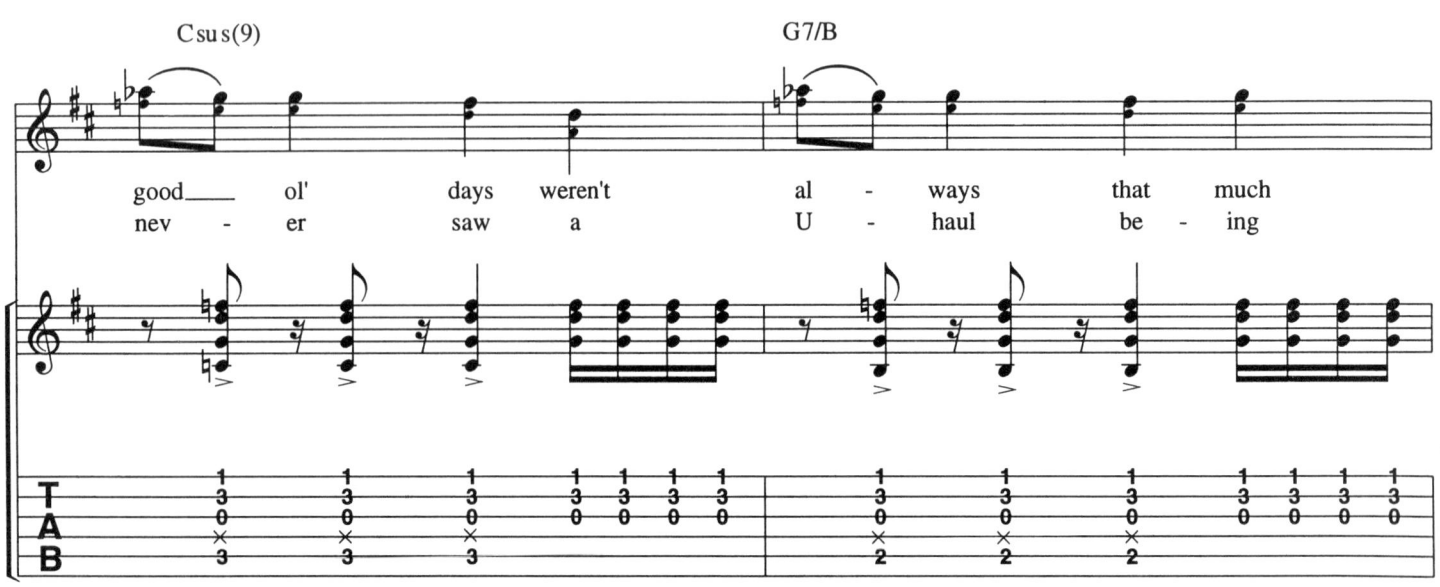

Csus(9)
G7/B
G5
bet - ter, yeah.
pulled be - hind a... Pulled be - hind a hearse.
'Cause I'm a
Chorus:
F5
N.C.
G5
N.C.
cyn - i - cal. Well, I ain't no - thing but a cyn - i - cal It don't take much to be a
Cyn - i - cal Fuck. Cyn - i - cal Fuck.
P.M.
F5 N.C. A♭5 N.C. G5
N.C.
cyn - i - cal. All you need is what to be a
All you need is love.
P.M.

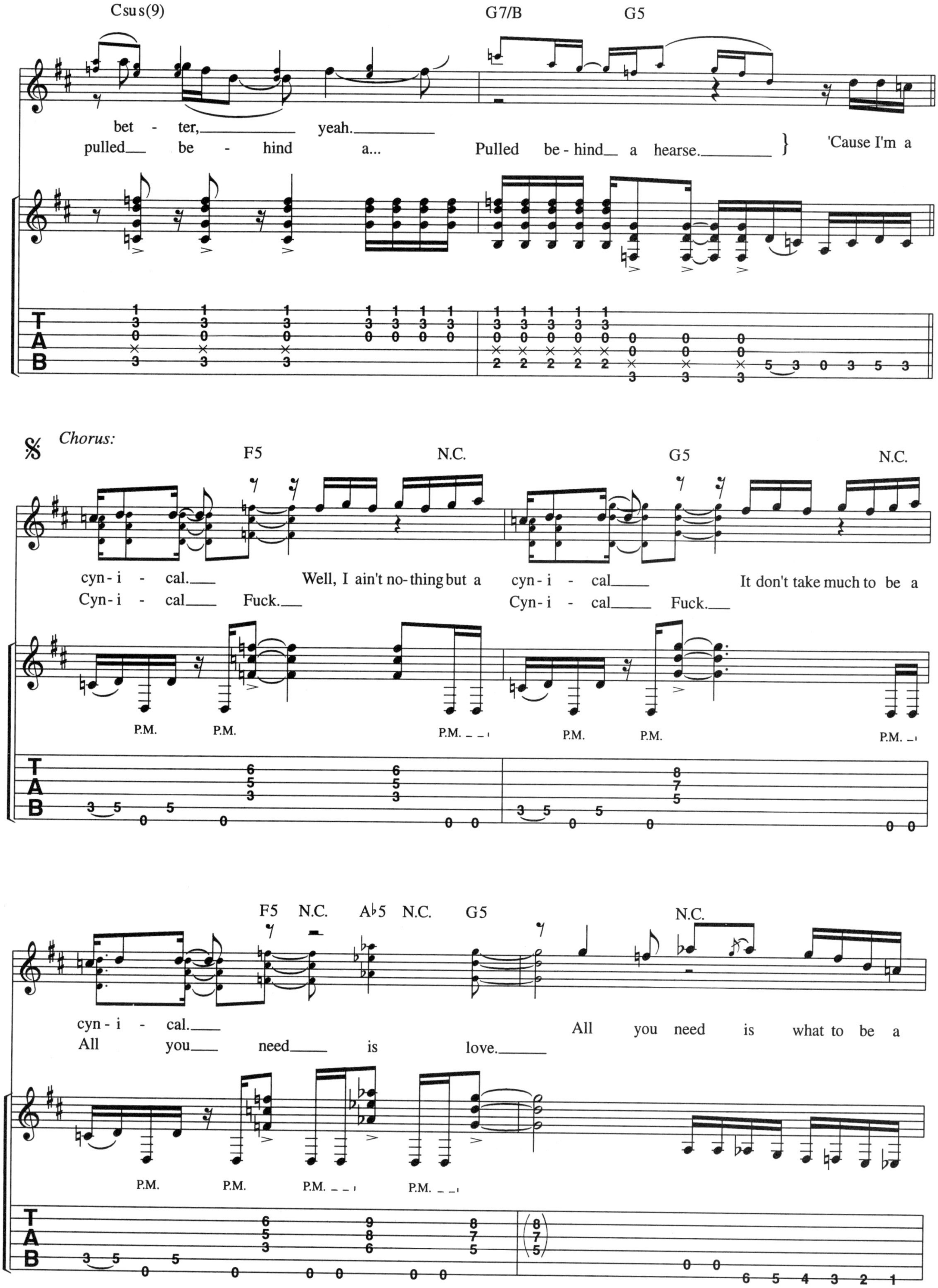

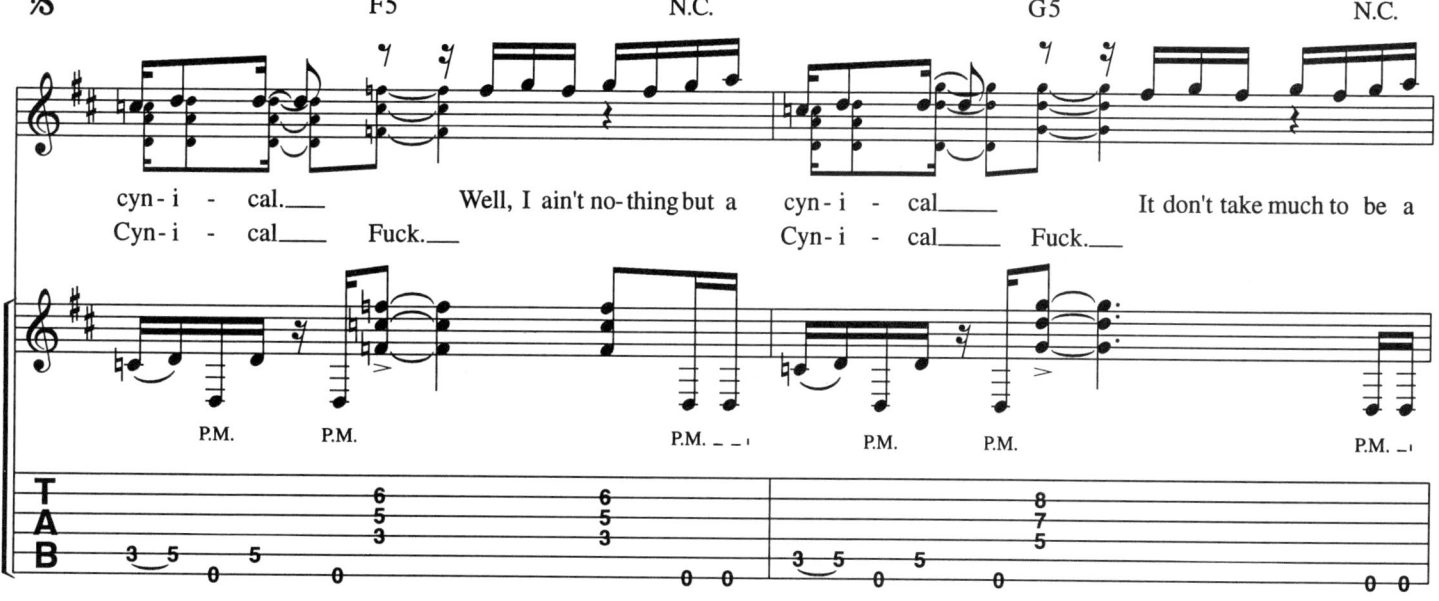

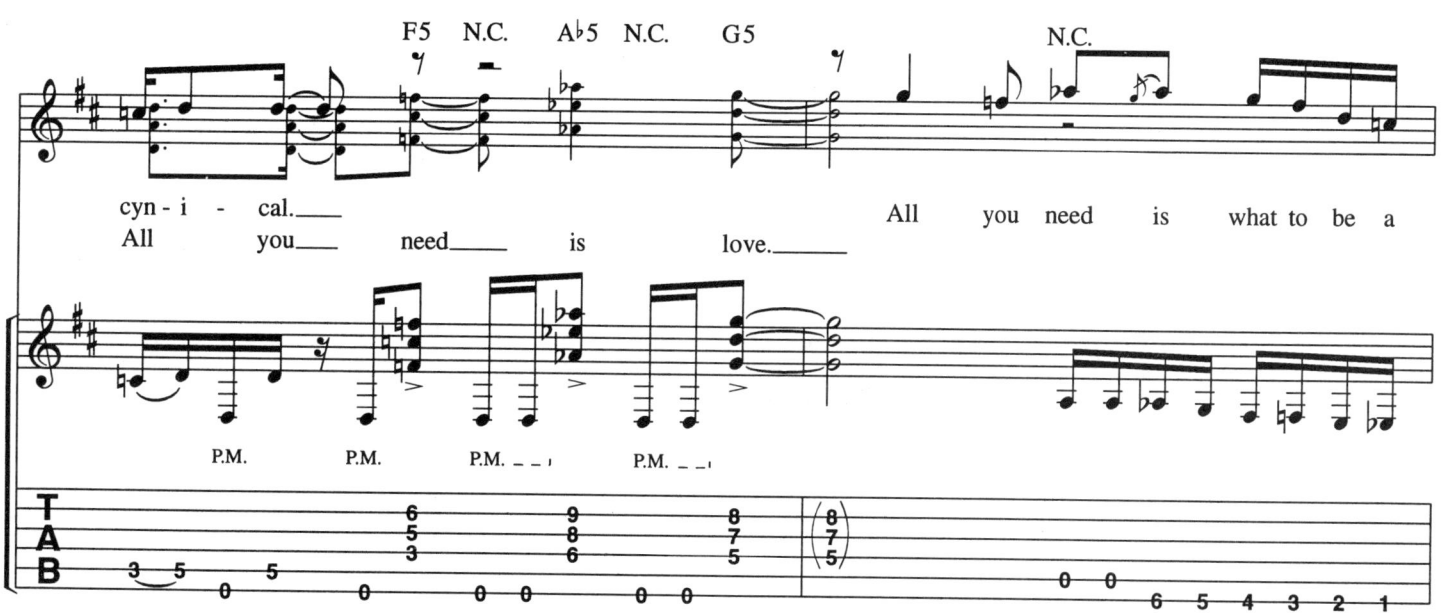

20

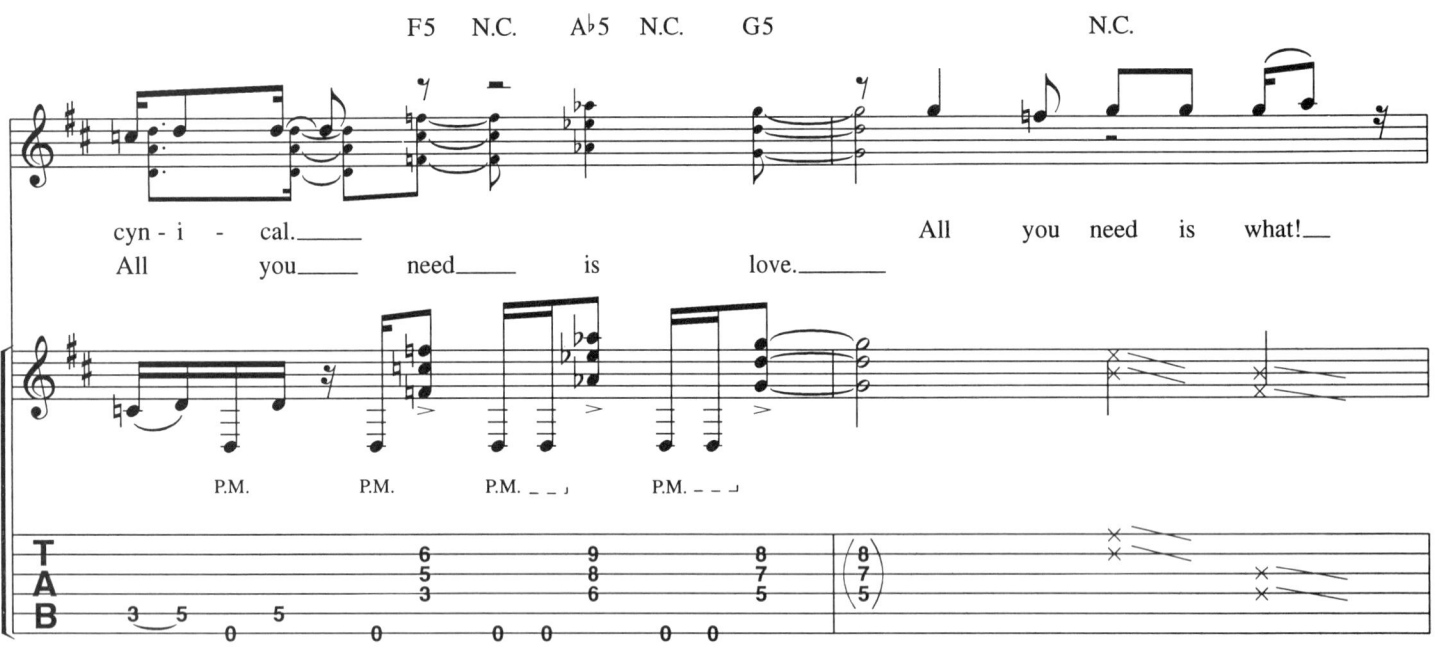
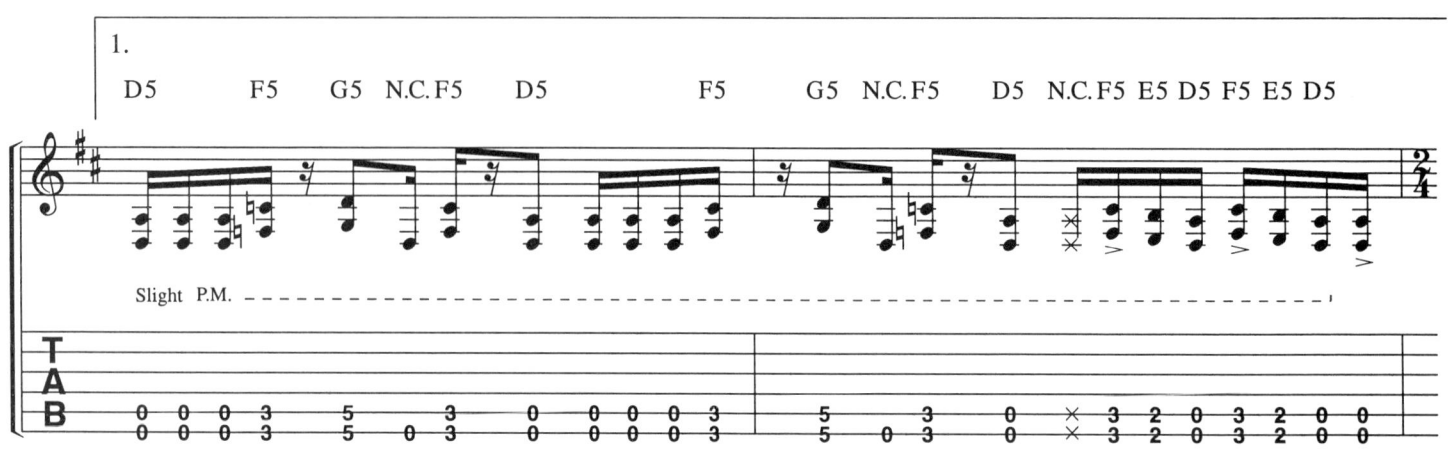

Cynical - 12 - 5
PG9515

22

Cynical - 12 - 7
PG9515

24

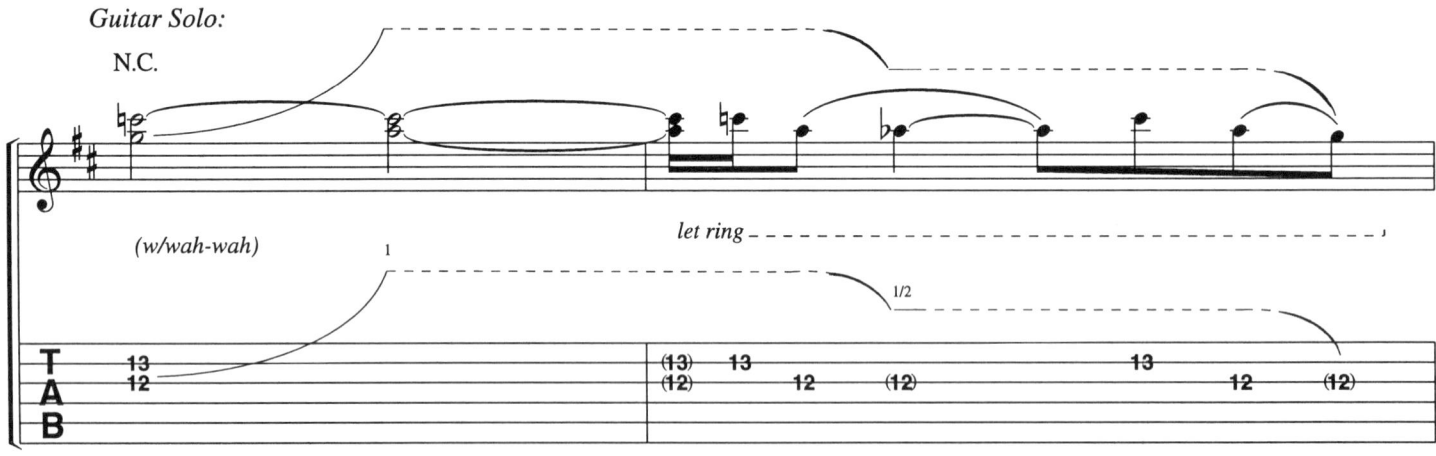

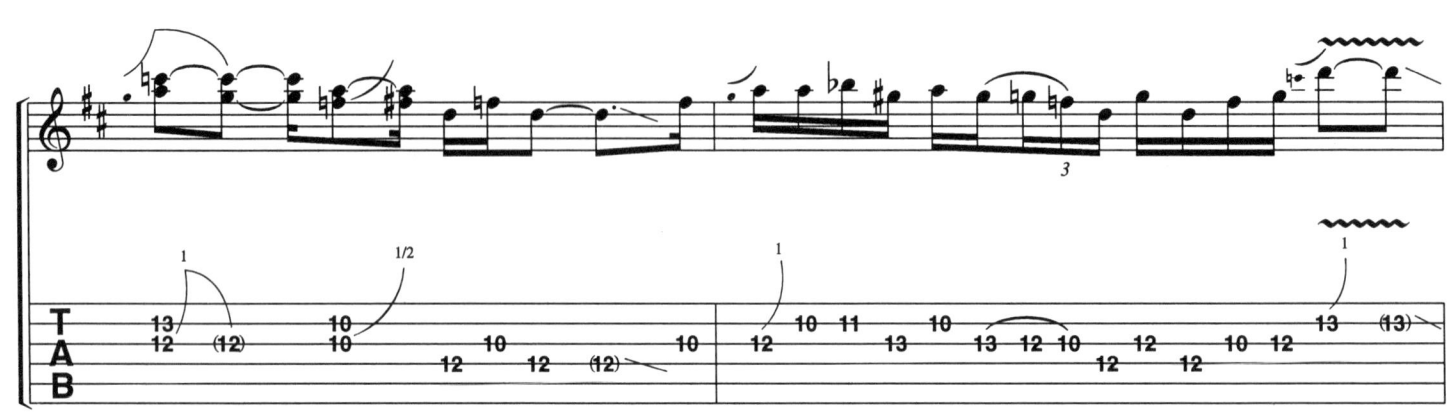

Cynical - 12 - 9
PG9515

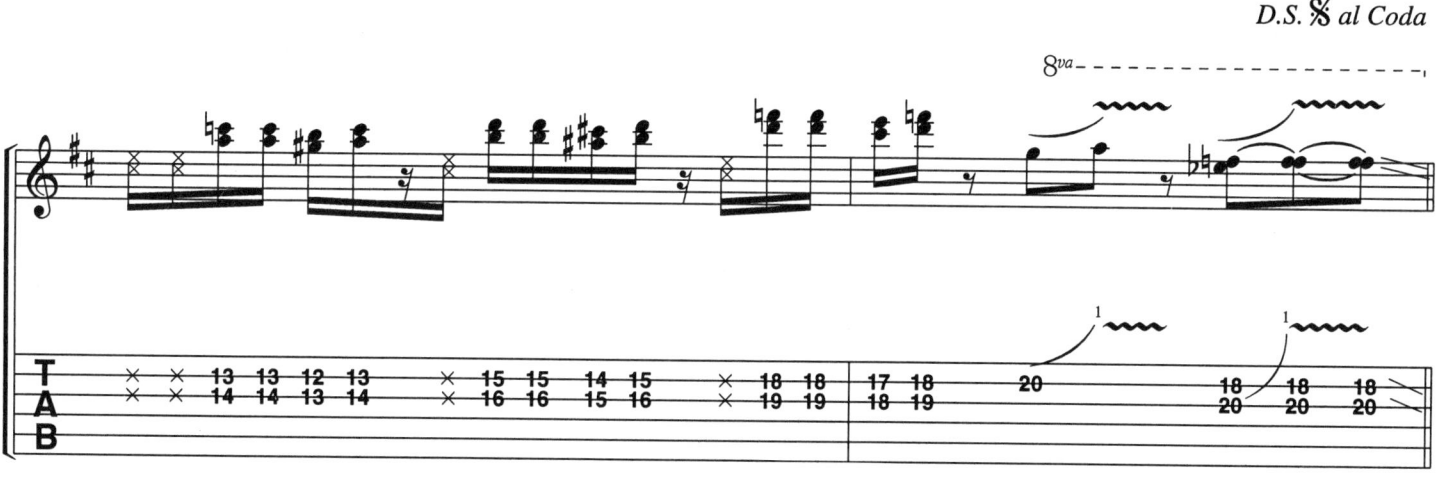

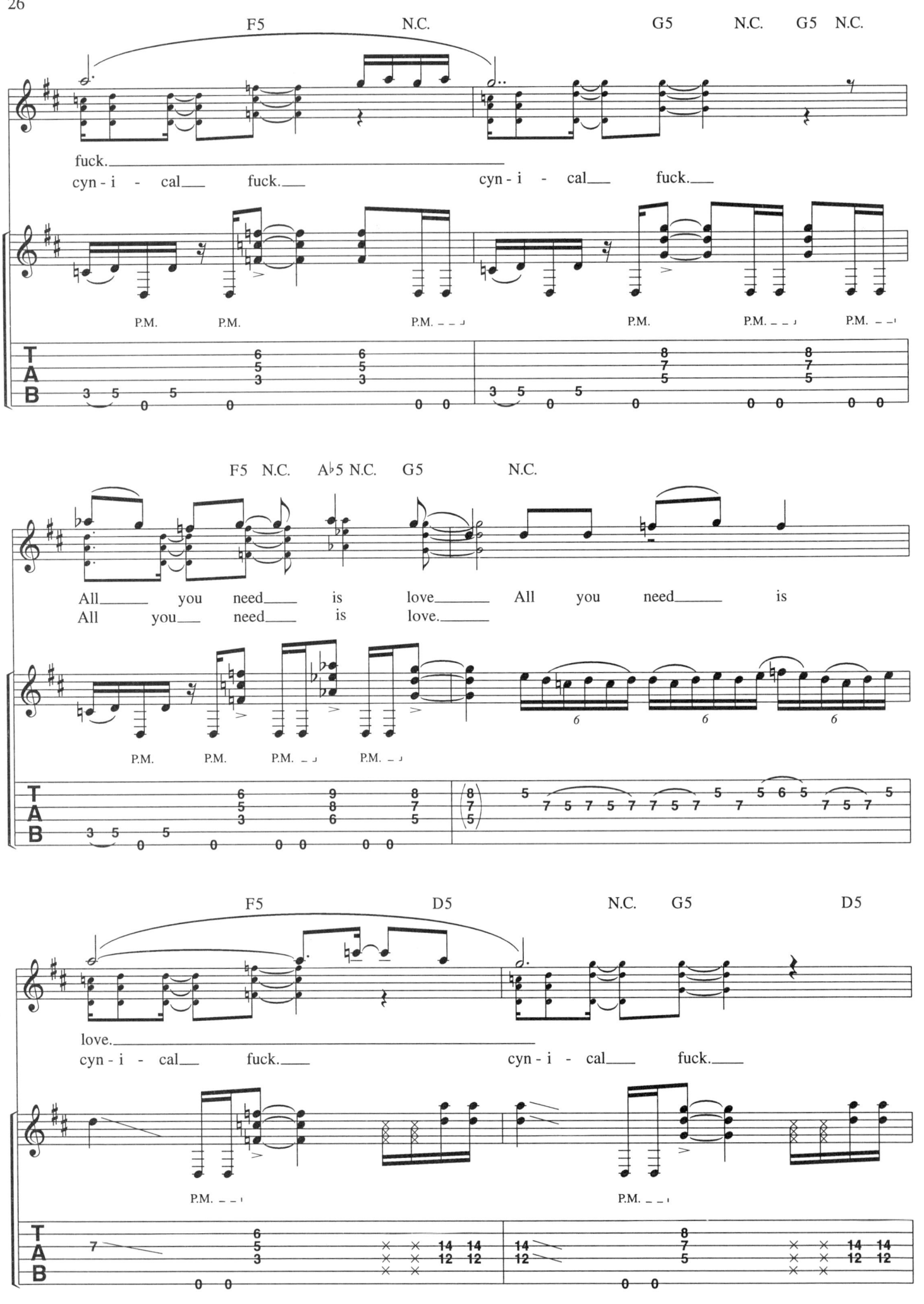

unconditionally

Words and Music by
NUNO BETTENCOURT/GARY CHERONE

All gtrs. tune down 1/2 step:
- ⑥ = E♭   ③ = G♭
- ⑤ = A♭   ② = B♭
- ④ = D♭   ① = E♭

Gtrs. 1 & 2: 6th string = D♭

Moderately slow rock ♩ = 78

Intro:
Gtr. 1 (Acoustic)

Unconditionally - 10 - 1
PG9515

Copyright © 1995 COLOR ME BLIND MUSIC (ASCAP)
All Rights Administered by ALMO MUSIC CORP. (ASCAP) for the World Under License from FUNKY METAL MUSIC, INC.
International Copyright Secured   Made in U.S.A.   All Rights Reserved

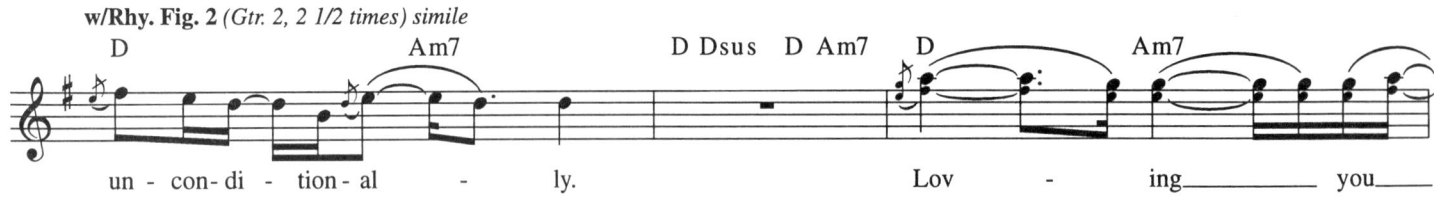

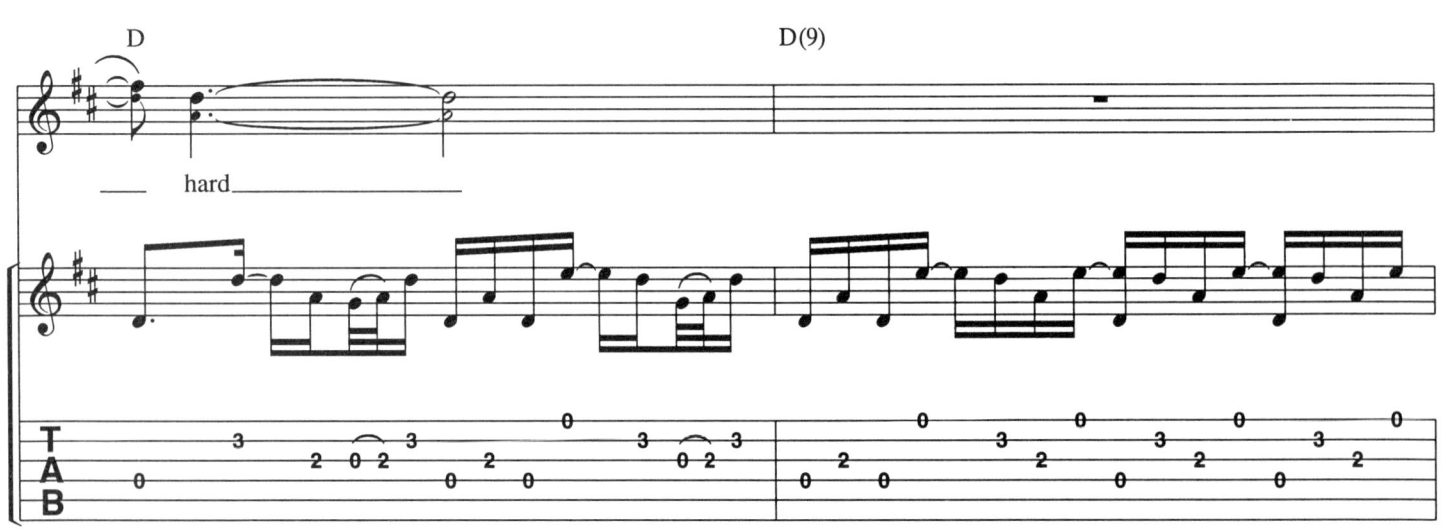

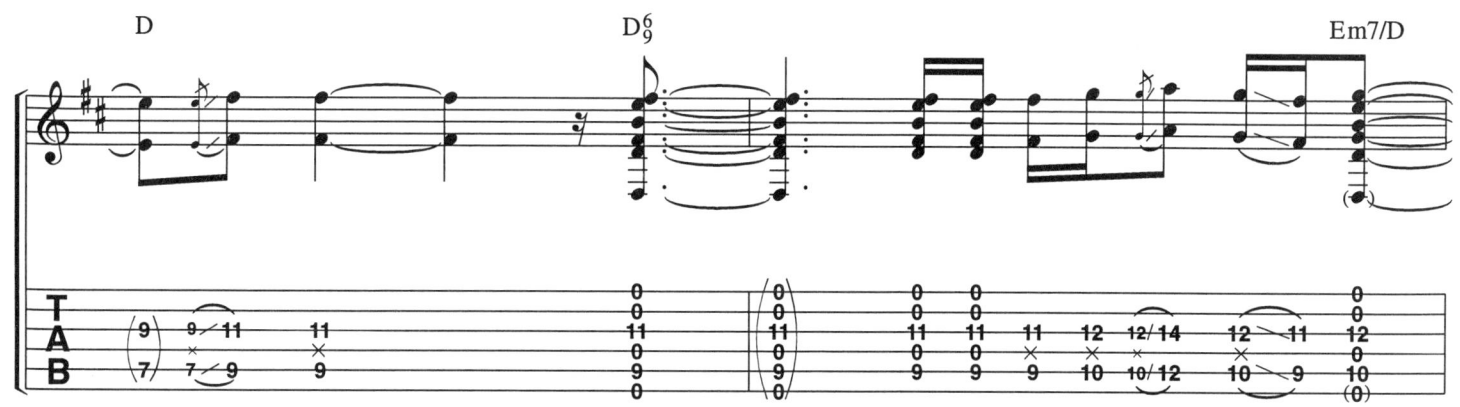
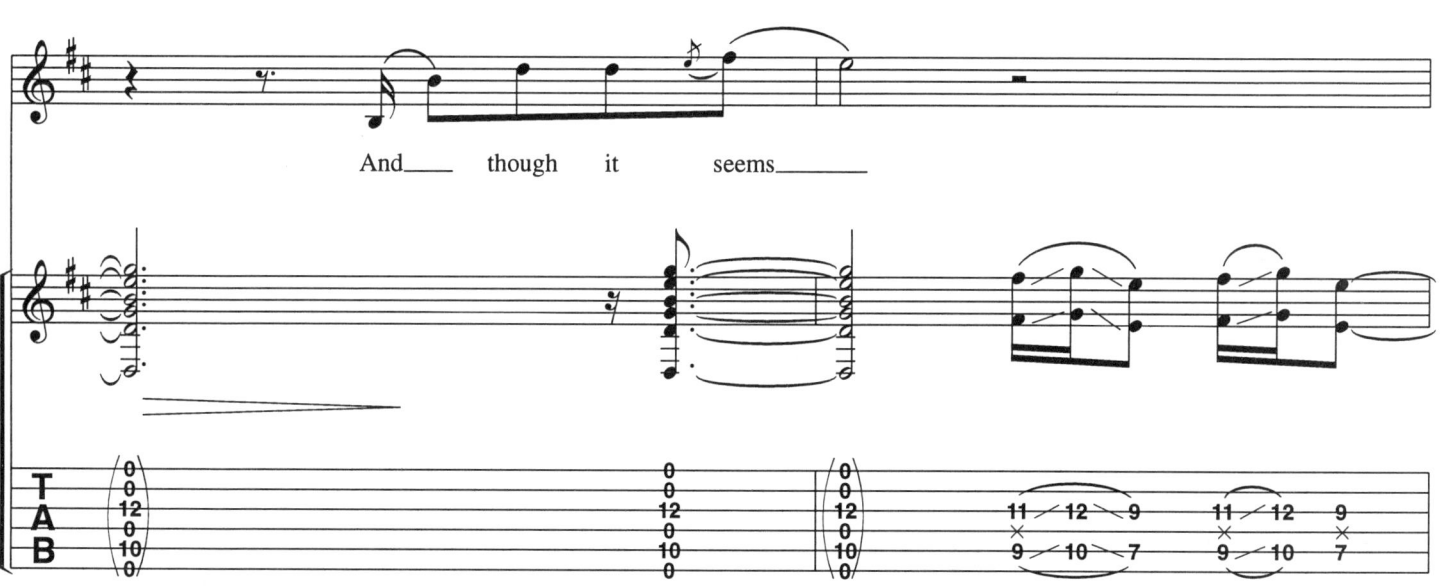

And though it seems

im-pos-si-ble

Unconditionally - 10 - 6
PG9515

34

Unconditionally - 10 - 7
PG9515

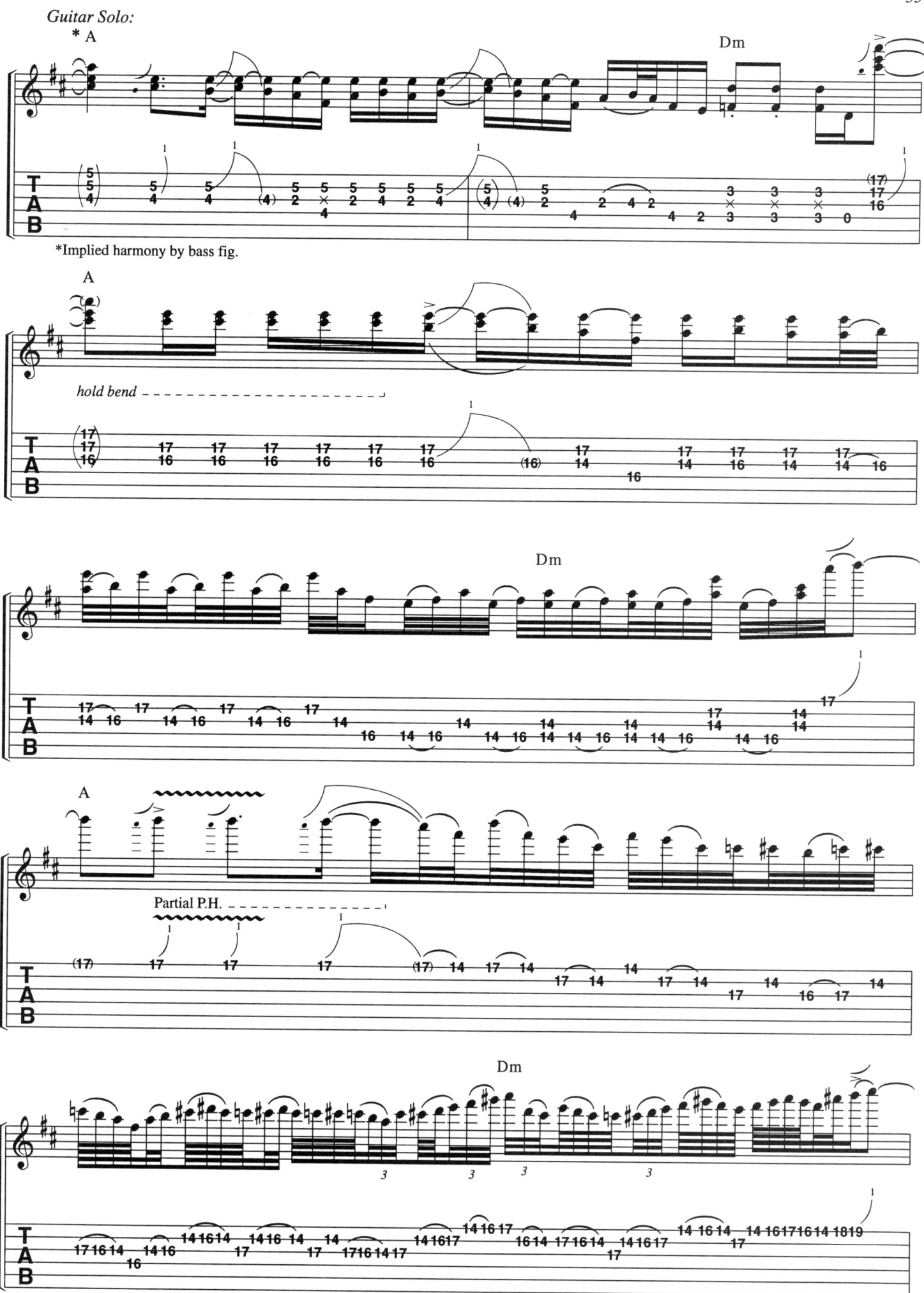

36

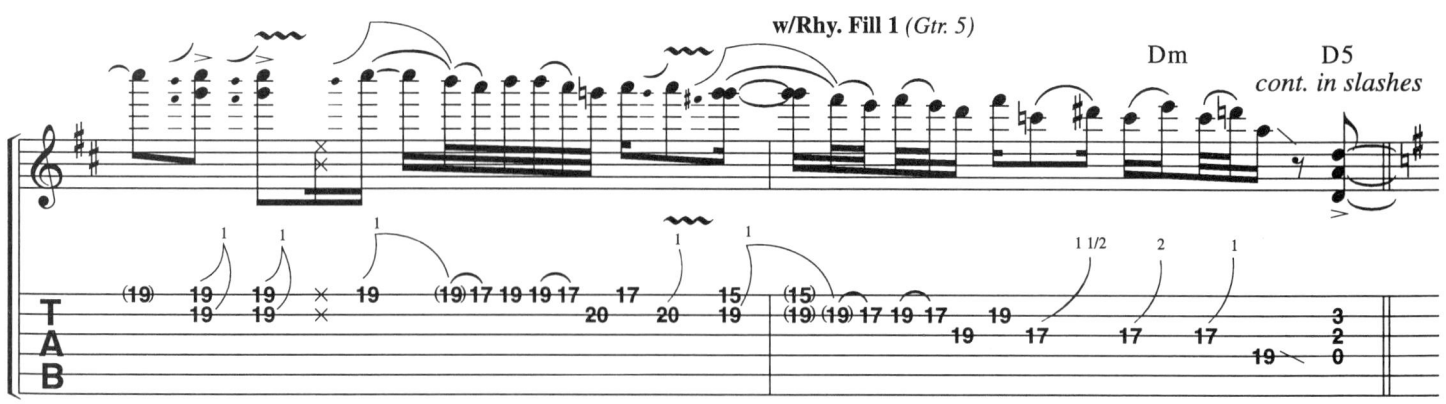

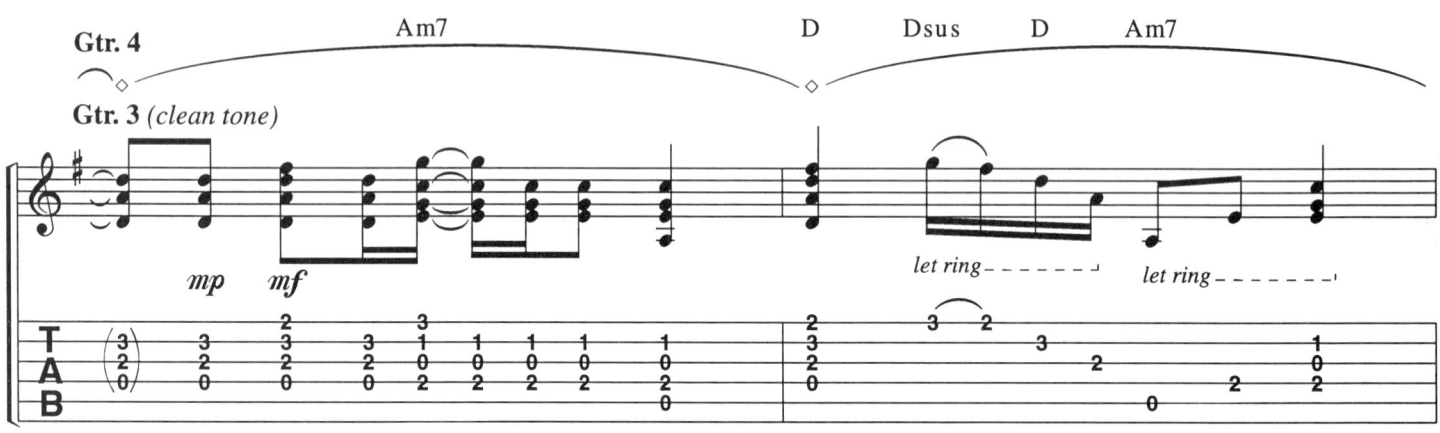

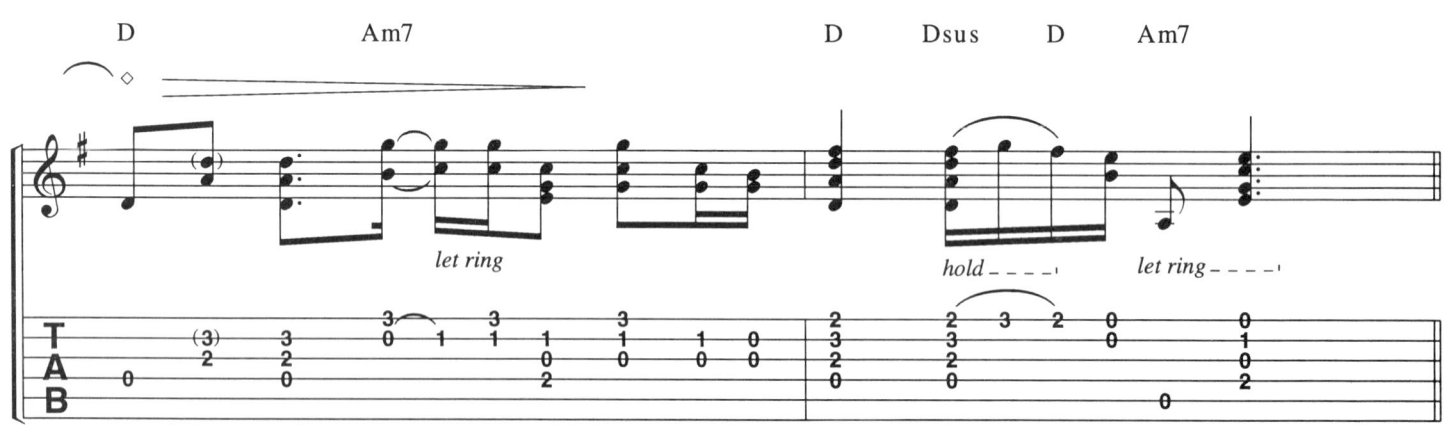

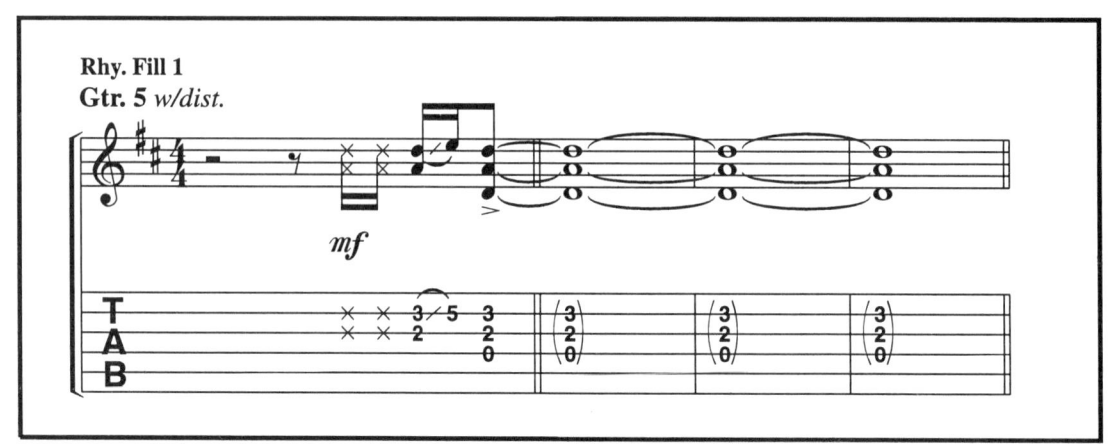

Unconditionally - 10 - 9
PG9515

Outro Chorus:
D5
Am7
D
Dsus
D
Am7
Lov - ing you
Gtrs. 2 & 3
Rhy. Fig. 3
let ring
D5
Am7
B♭/F
F
B♭
F
(G) D5
un - con - di - tion - al - ly, it's what I want to be. Lov -
end Rhy. Fig. 3
let ring
w/Rhy. Fig. 3 (Gtrs. 2 & 3, 1 1/2 times) simile
Am7
D Dsus D Am7
D
Am7
ing you un - con - di - tion - al - ly it's
B♭/F
F B♭ F
(G)
D
Am7
D
Dsus
D
Am7
what I want to be. It's lov - ing you is
B♭/F
F
D
what I want to be. It's what you are to me.
Gtr. 2
let ring

evilangelist

Words and Music by
NUNO BETTENCOURT/GARY CHERONE

All gtrs. tune down 1/2 step:

⑥ = E♭ ③ = G♭
⑤ = A♭ ② = B♭
④ = D♭ ① = E♭

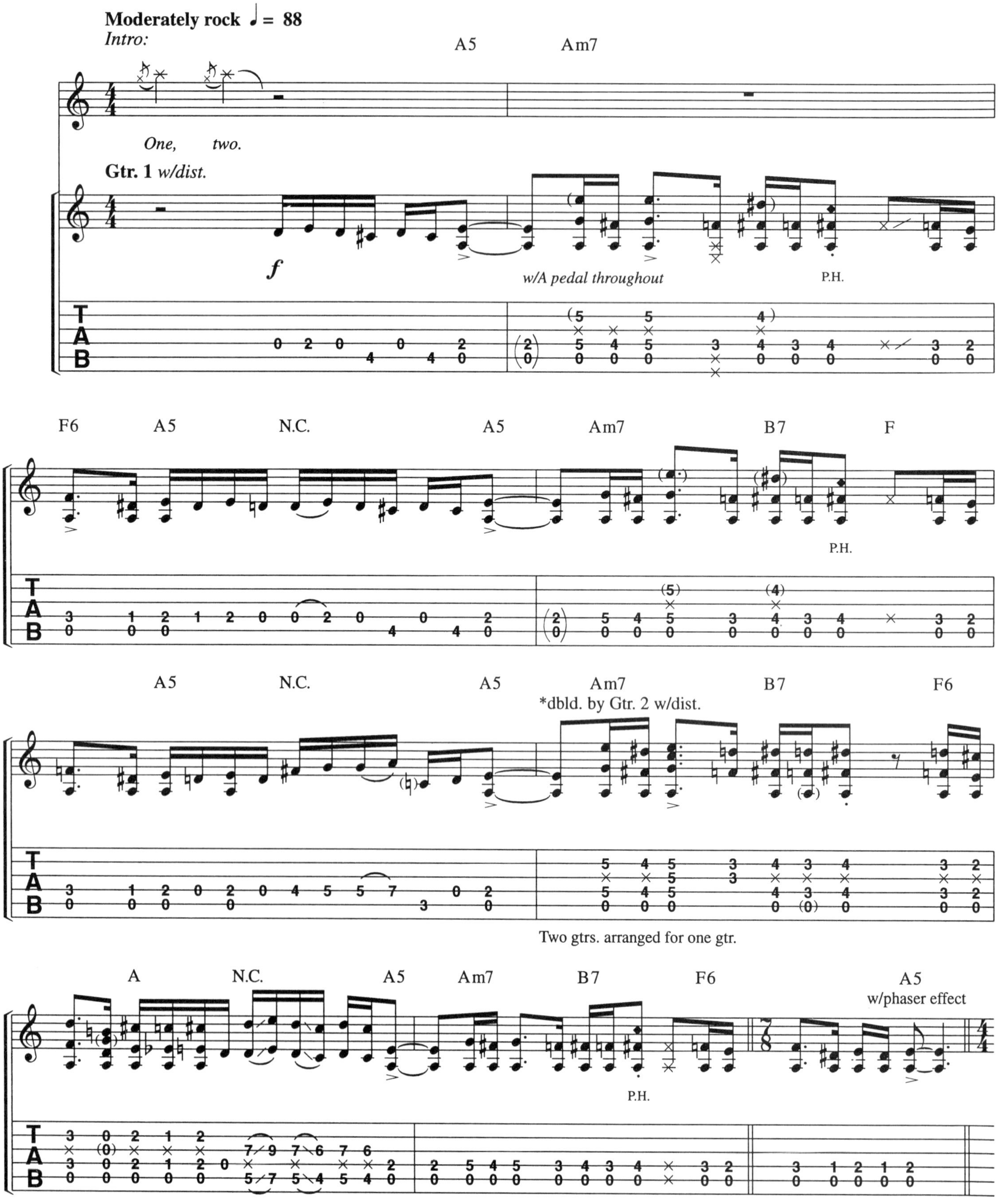

Verse:
Gtr. 2 tacet
*Am7
D5/A
A
Am7
1. Lit - tle lamb come out of the rain.
2. See additional lyrics.
Rhy. Fig. 1
Partial P.M. throughout
*Basic harmony.
A5
Am7
A5
D/A
Am7
A5
A
You'll catch your death in the cold.
end Rhy. Fig.1
Am7
D5/A
A5
Am7
A help - ing hand to come ease the pain.
1/2
1/2

40

41

N.C. A5 Am7 B7 F6 A5
In what god you trust.
fdbk.
P.H.
Verse:
w/Rhy. Fig. 1 (Gtr. 1)
Am7 D5/A A Am7
3. Close your eyes while I hyp - no - tize
A5 Am7 A5 D/A Am7 A5 A Am Am6 Am Am6
a friend in need to con - fess. (A) you've been de - nied,
Am Am6 Am7 D Am7 Am6 Am7
the cock crowed thrice. Sur - rend - er

A5
Am7
B7
all you pos - sess.
P.H.
F6
N.C.
Chorus:
w/Rhy. Fig. 2 (Gtr. 1, 4 times) simile
N.C.
(E)
E - vil - an - ge - list,
E - vil - an - ge - list.
your name is on my list.
Yeah, I'm your e - vil - an - ge - list.
E - vil - an - ge - list.
Well, I was be-trayed by a kiss.
E - vil - an - ge - list.

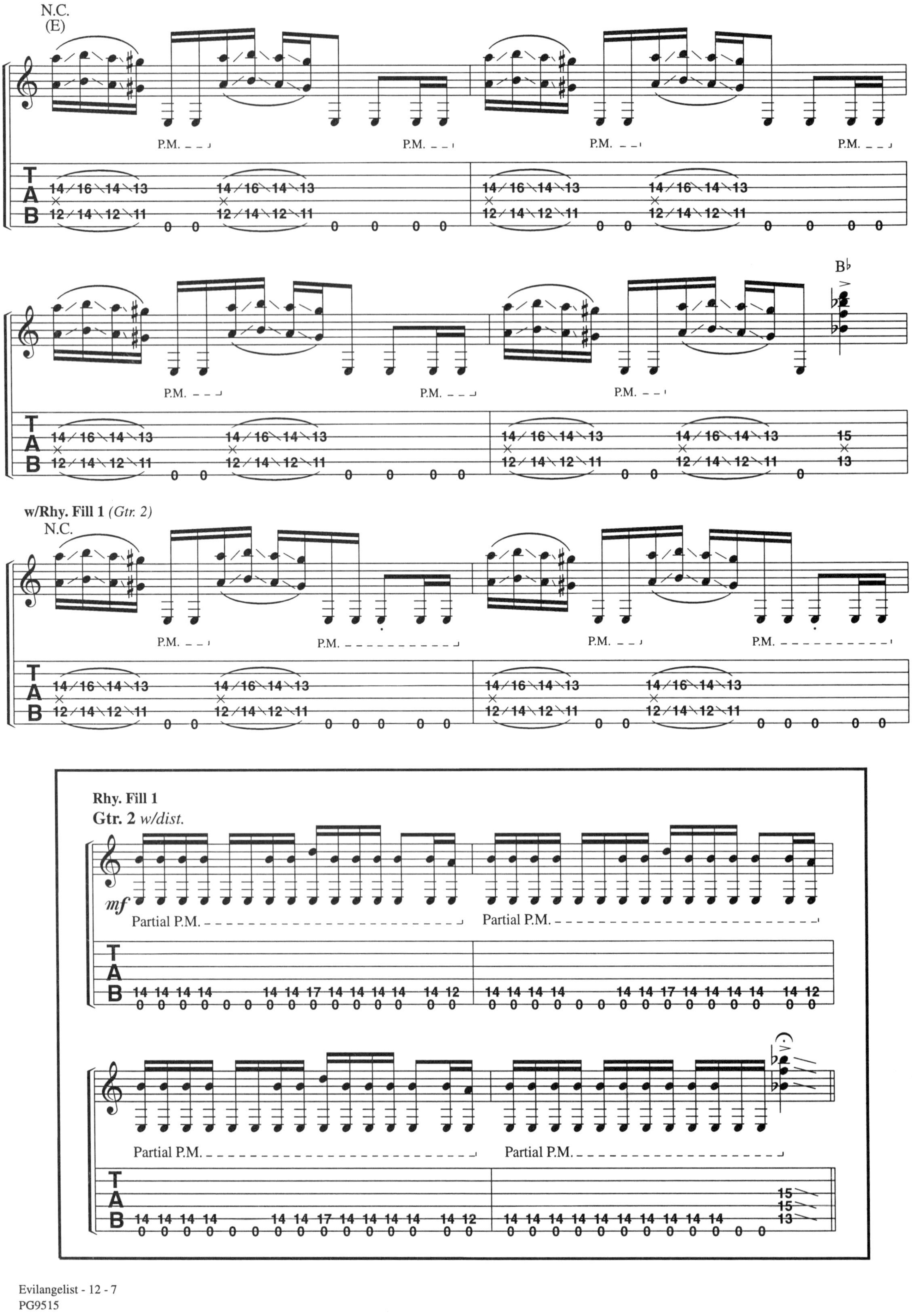
N.C.
(E)
P.M.
B♭
w/Rhy. Fill 1 (Gtr. 2)
N.C.
Rhy. Fill 1
Gtr. 2 w/dist.
mf
Partial P.M.

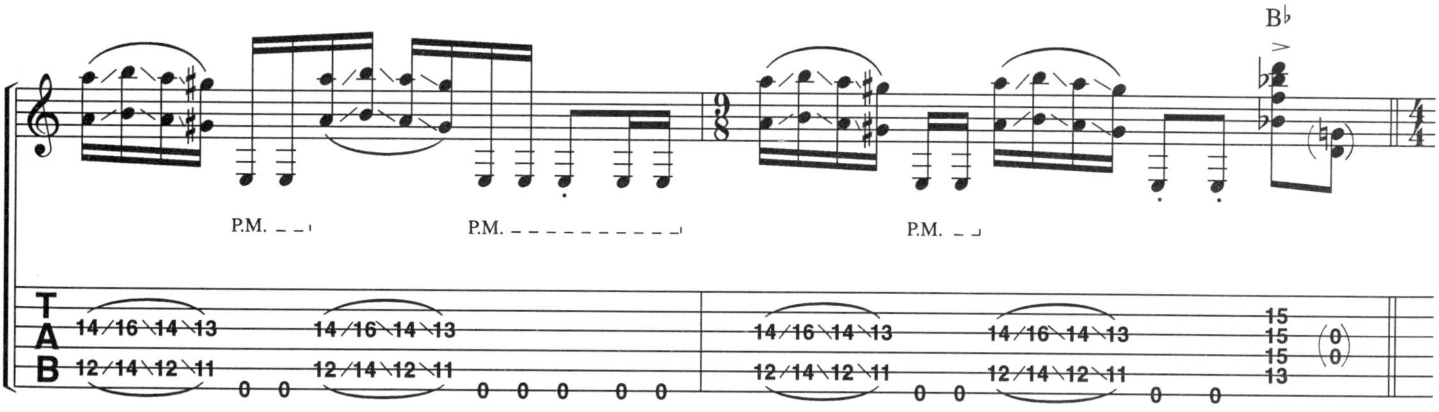

Guitar Solo:
***Gtr. 2** w/dist.*

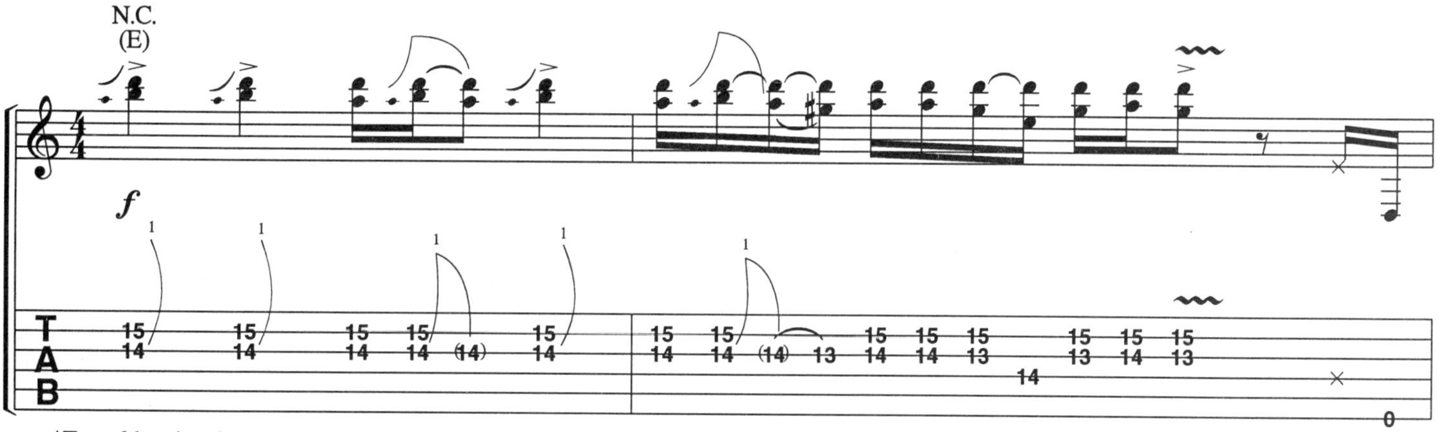

*Tune 6th string down to D.

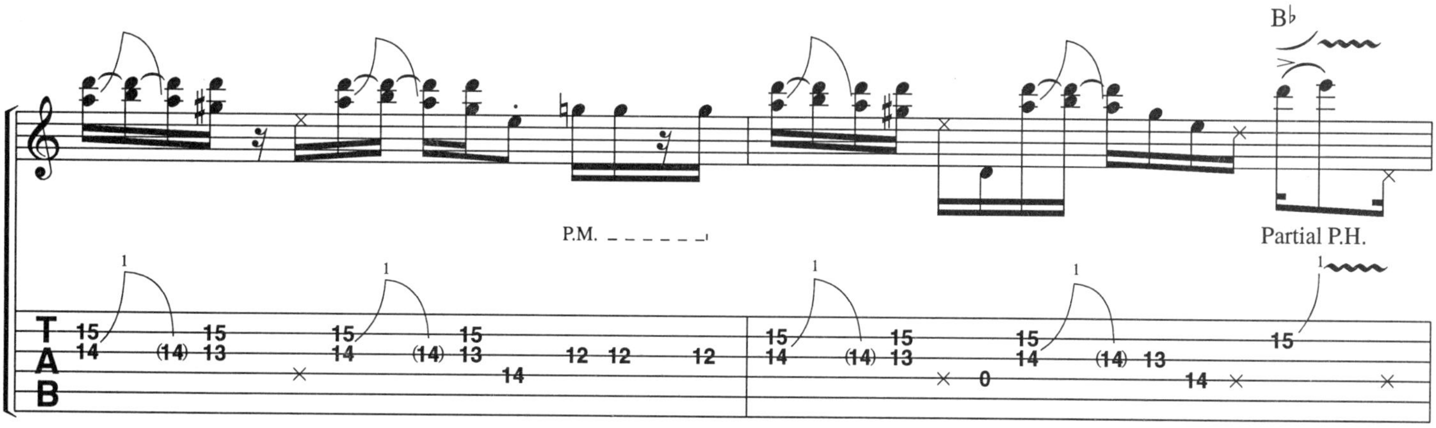

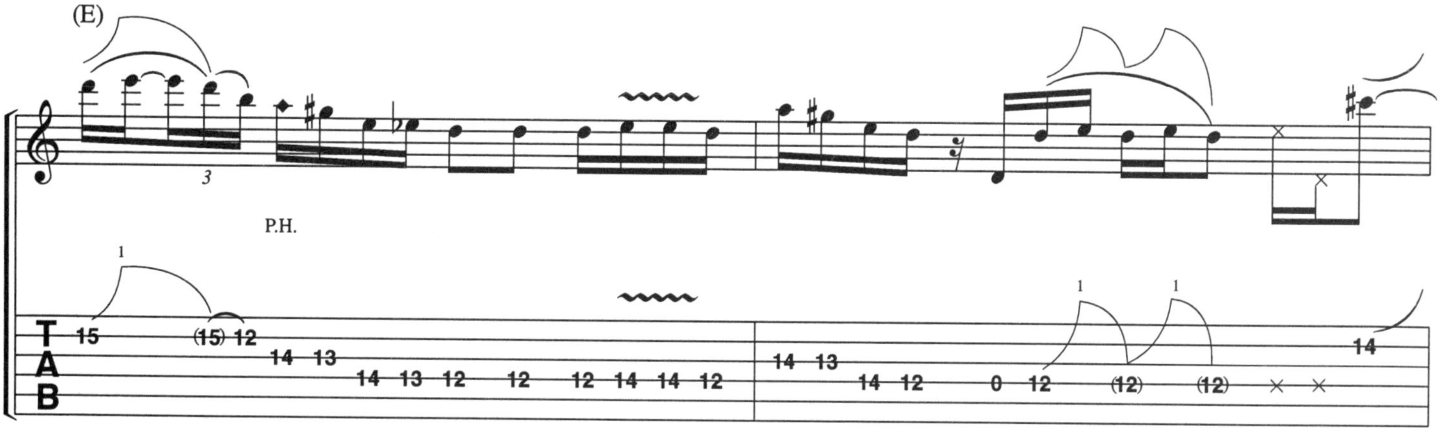

Bridge:

So____ man - y claim_____ to come in thy name_____ prom - is - ing peace____

P.M. single notes on 5th string

let ring_____

let ring___

Evilangelist - 12 - 9
PG9515

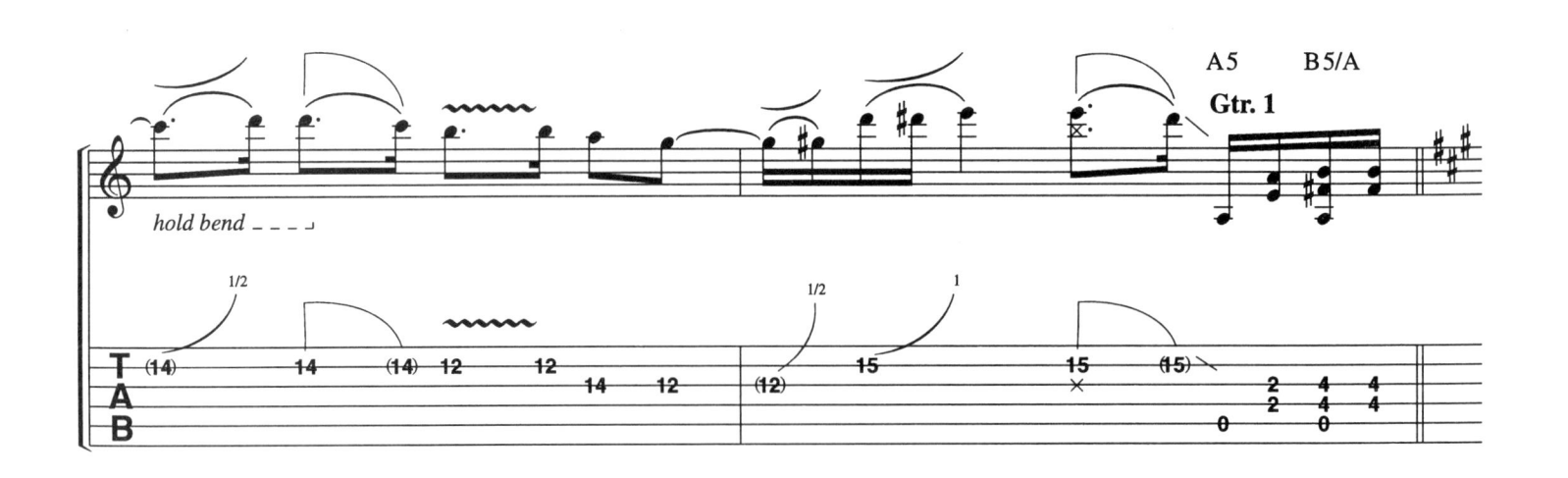

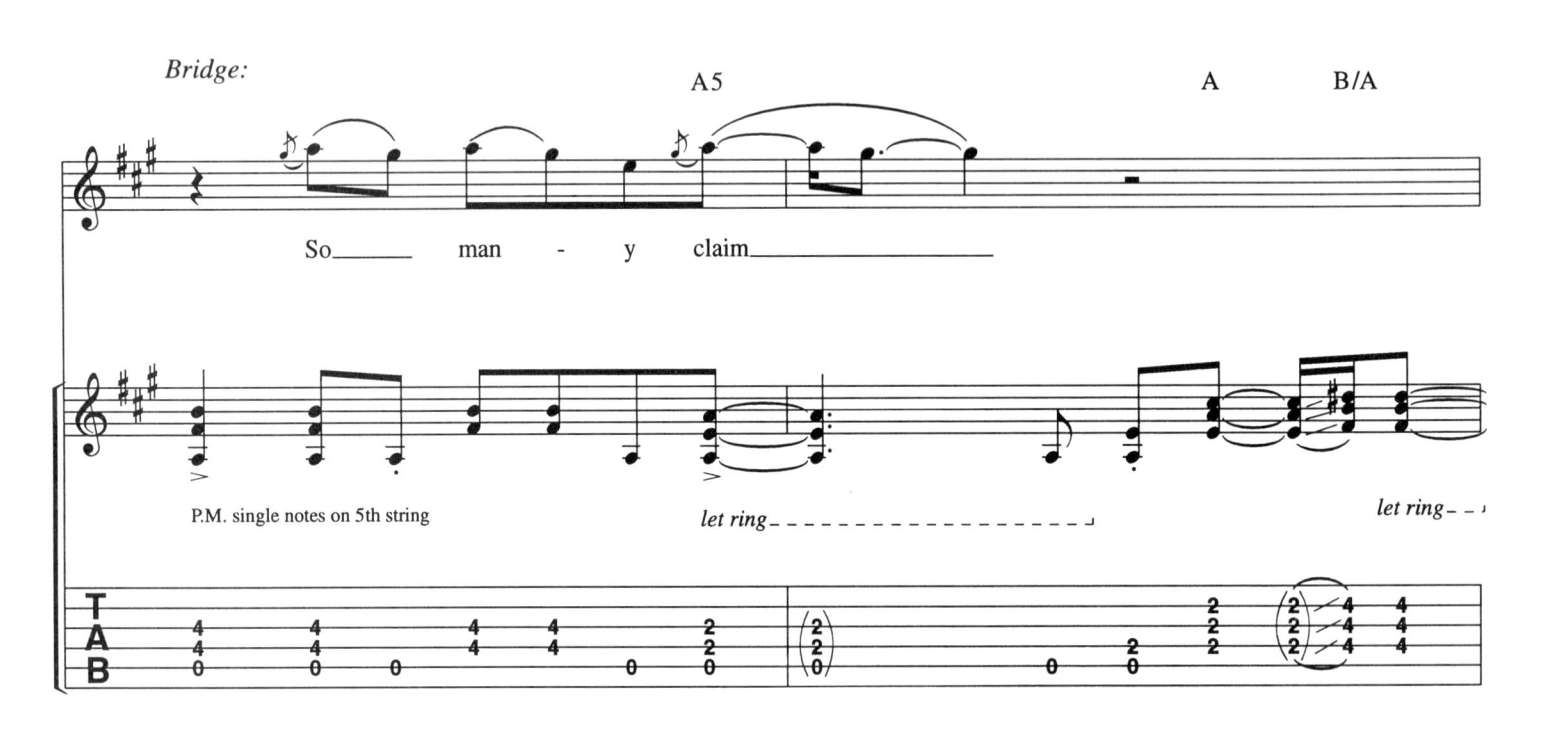

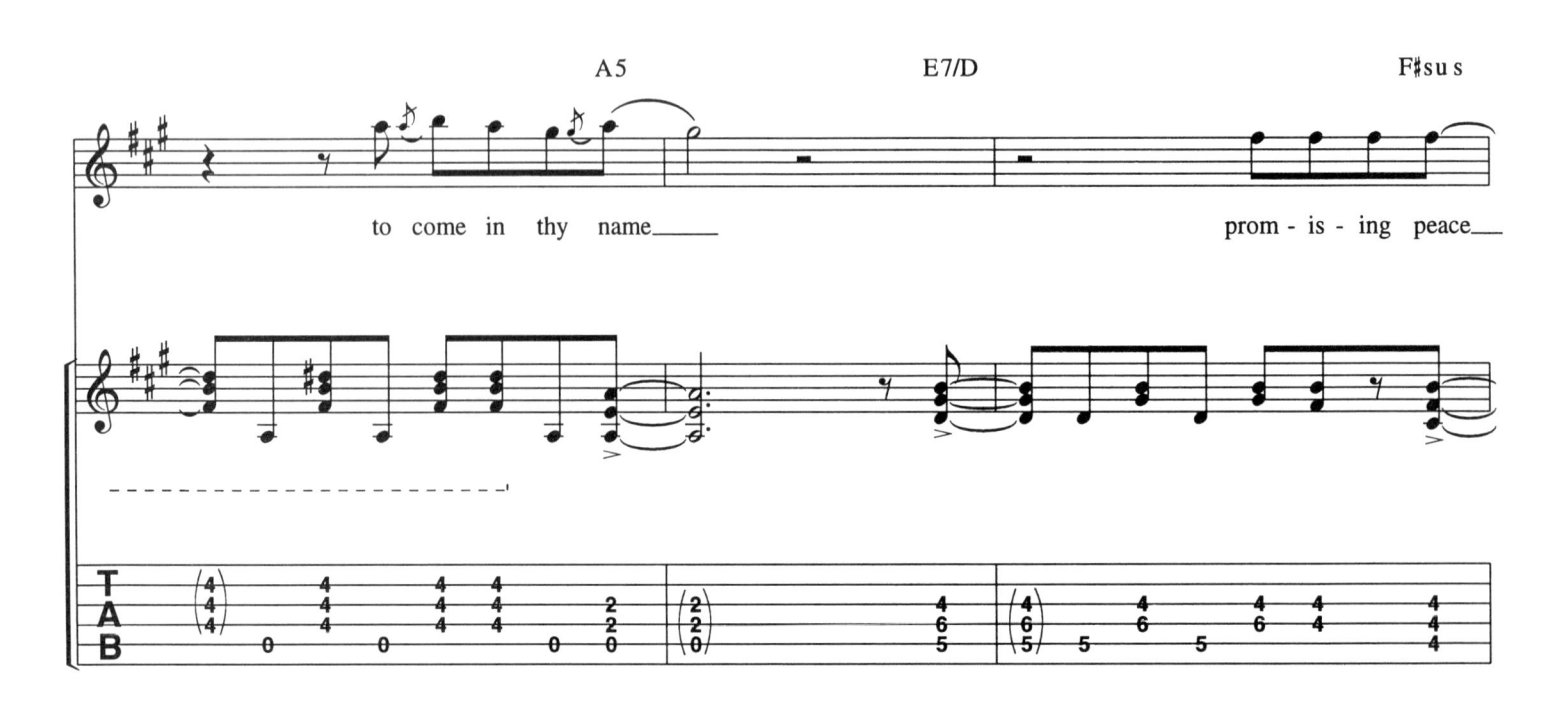

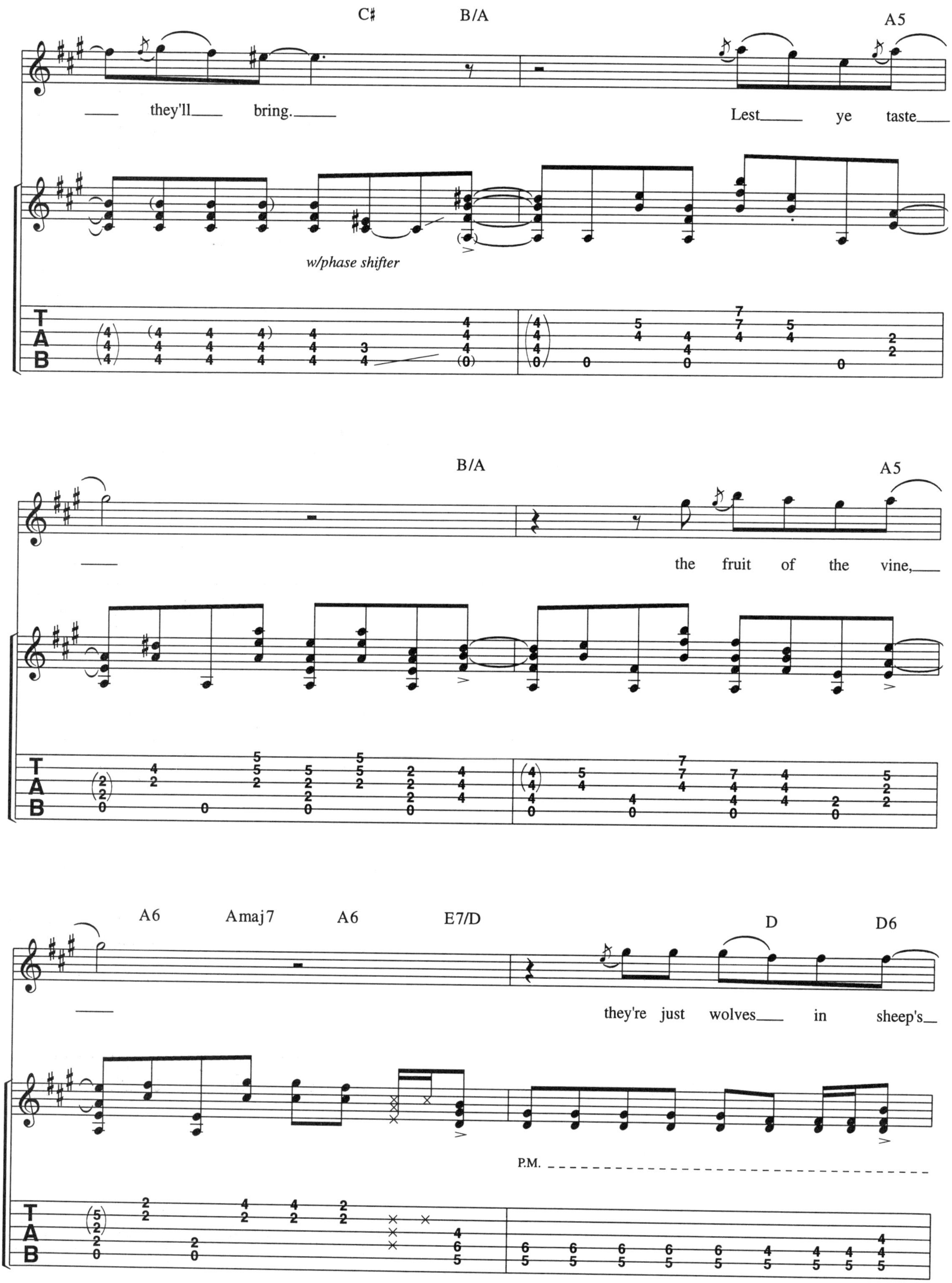
C♯
B/A
A5
they'll bring.
Lest ye taste
w/phase shifter
TAB
B/A
A5
the fruit of the vine,
TAB
A6
Amaj7
A6
E7/D
D
D6
they're just wolves in sheep's
P.M.
TAB

48

Bkgd. vcl: E - vil.

Outro:
N.C.
(E)

In_____ what god you trust.____

w/Rhy. Fill 1 *(Gtr. 1, last 2 bars only) simile*
N.C.
(E)

Verse 2:
I can be a watch towering light,
For those of you who can't see.
I'll separate the truth from the lies,
Blind faithful come follow me.

leave me alone

Words and Music by
NUNO BETTENCOURT/GARY CHERONE/MIKE MAGNINI

All gtrs. tuned down 1/2 step:
- ⑥ = E♭   ③ = G♭
- ⑤ = A♭   ② = B♭
- ④ = D♭   ① = E♭

B♭5   E5

Moderately slow rock ♩ = 74

Intro Verse:

As for this song, I'll set the mood. There's nothing wrong, prefer solitude. Alone to think of what (a) I don't know. Deeper I sink, the further I'll go.

Gtr. 1 w/dist. and heavy reverb effect
Partial P.M. throughout unless stated otherwise

*basic harmony w/E pedal

Leave Me Alone - 9 - 1
PG9515

Copyright © 1995 COLOR ME BLIND MUSIC and MIKE MAGNINI PUBLISHING DESIGNEE
All Rights Administered by ALMO MUSIC CORP. (ASCAP) Throughout the World Under License from FUNKY METAL MUSIC, INC.
International Copyright Secured   Made in U.S.A.   All Rights Reserved

doubled by Gtr. 2 w/dist
E
w/o reverb effect
*P.M. open single notes on 6th string.
D
A
2. Noth - ing to fear,
Verse:
E
no need to hide.
I'm al - read- y there,
(Gtr. 2 tacet)
Gtr. 1
Rhy. Fig. 1
w/reverb effect
1/2
let ring
let ring
D
A
came in from out - side.
Safe in my
let ring
1/2

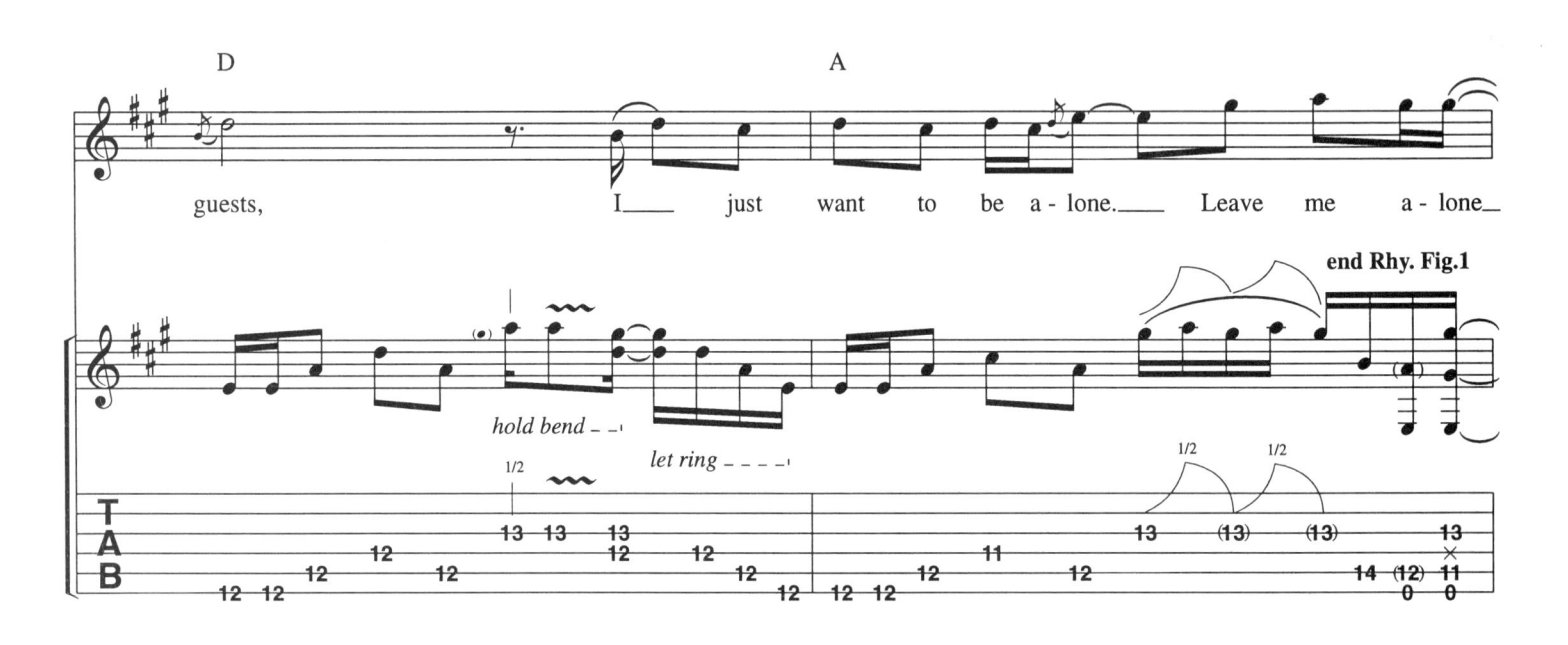

nest, my home sweet home, no in-vit-ed guests, I just want to be a-lone. Leave me a-lone

Chorus: leave me a-lone,

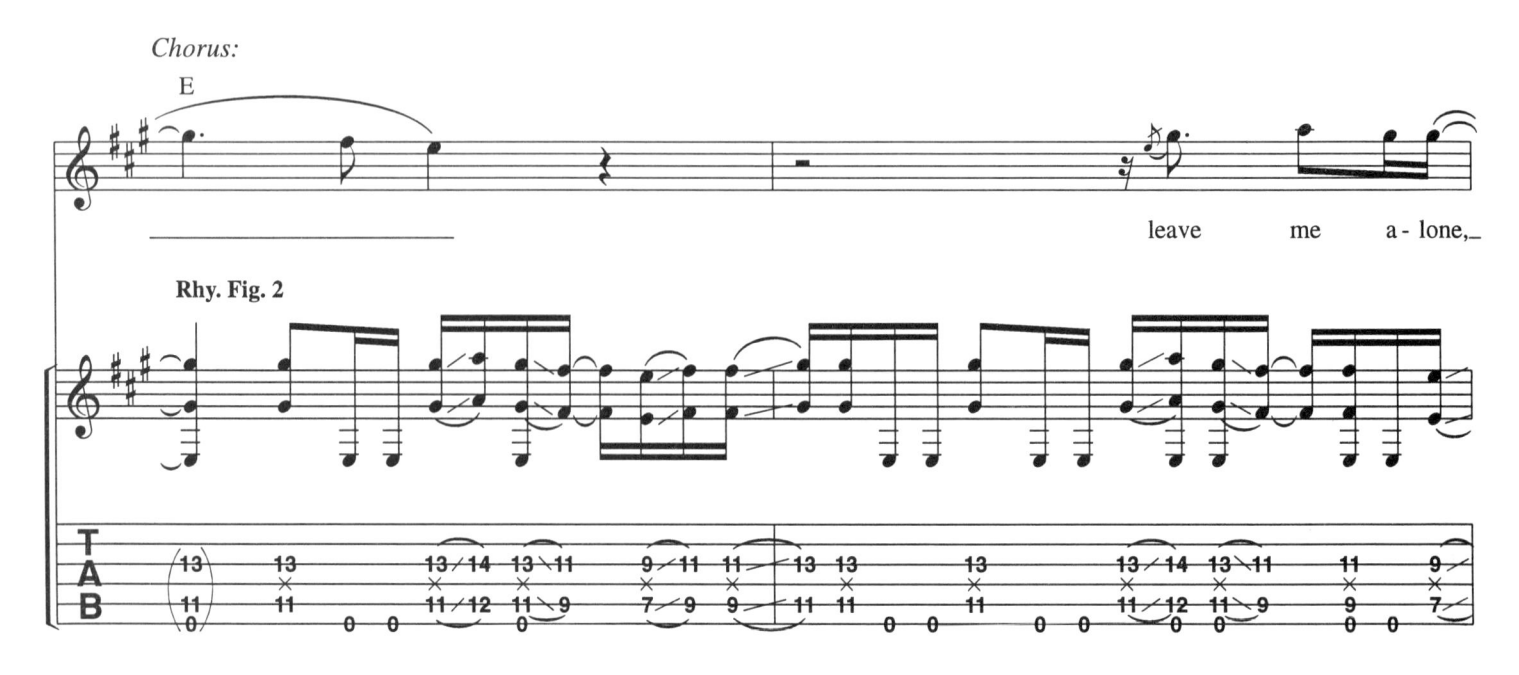

D
A
leave me a - lone.
end Rhy. Fig. 2
w/Rhy. Fig. 2 (Gtr. 2, 1st 3 meas.)
E
Wish you would leave me a - lone,
I wish you would leave me a - lone.
I just
D
Asus
A
Verse:
w/Rhy. Fig. 1 (Gtr. 1) simile
E
want to be a - lone
3. It's bet - ter this way, no one will get
Gtr. 1
hurt. If you stay a - way
D
I won't lose my shirt.
A
If I've be -
E
come (too) de - fen - sive,
I'm not the one
D
you're liv - ing with.

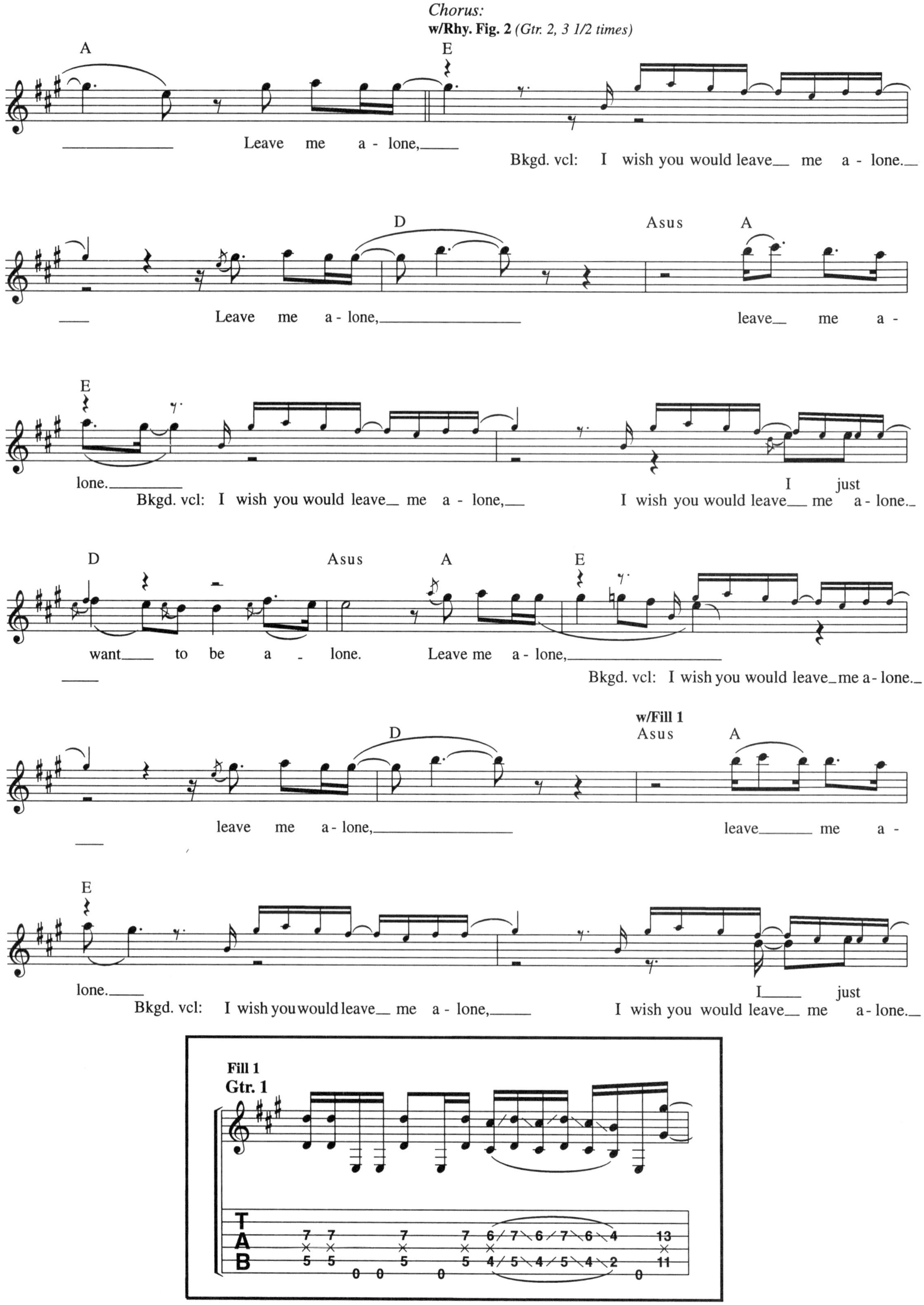
Chorus:
w/Rhy. Fig. 2 (Gtr. 2, 3 1/2 times)
A
E
Leave me a - lone,
Bkgd. vcl: I wish you would leave me a - lone.
D
Asus
A
Leave me a - lone,
leave me a -
E
lone.
Bkgd. vcl: I wish you would leave me a - lone,
I just
I wish you would leave me a - lone.
D
Asus
A
E
want to be a - lone.
Leave me a - lone,
Bkgd. vcl: I wish you would leave me a - lone.
w/Fill 1
D
Asus
A
leave me a - lone,
leave me a -
E
lone.
Bkgd. vcl: I wish you would leave me a - lone,
I just
I wish you would leave me a - lone.
Fill 1
Gtr. 1
T
A
B

Lyrics:
want to be a-lone. Leave me a-lone.

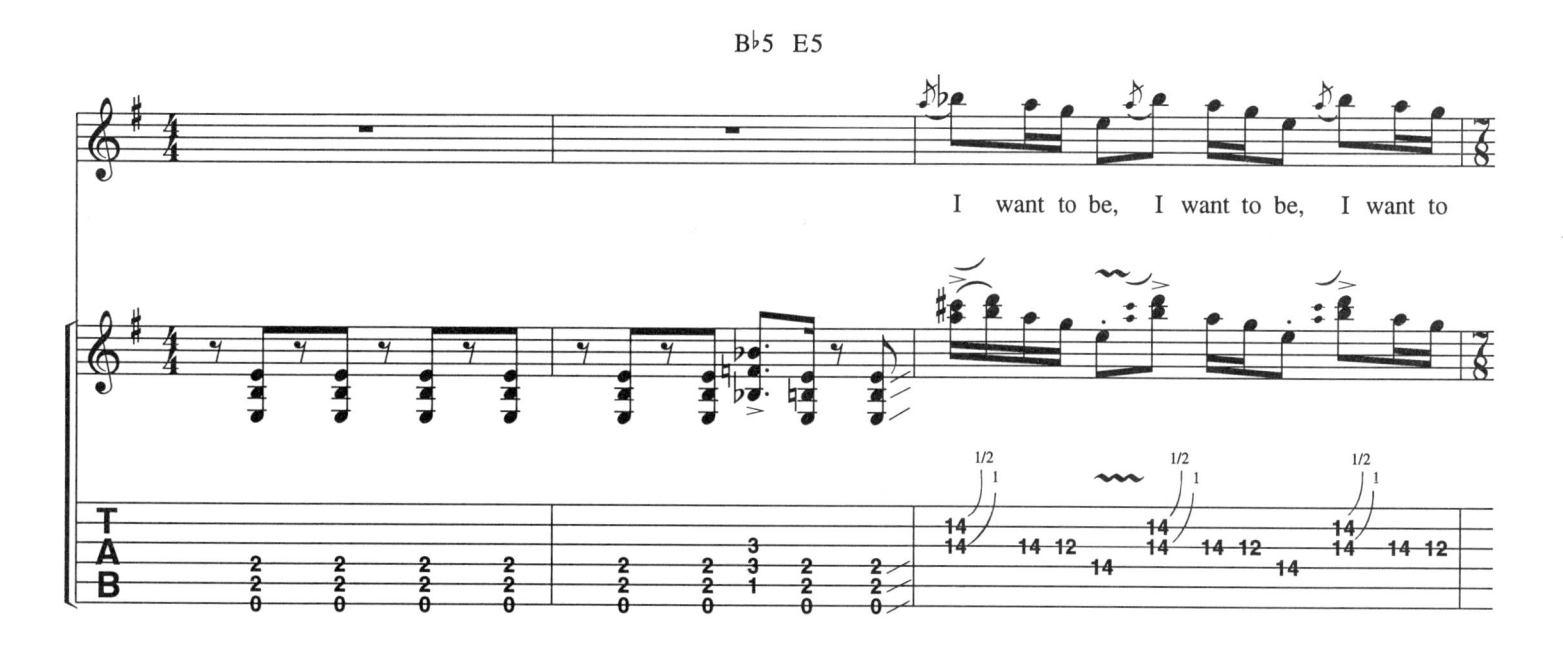

I want to be, I want to be, I want to be a-lone. I want to be, I want to be, I want to

Leave Me Alone - 9 - 6

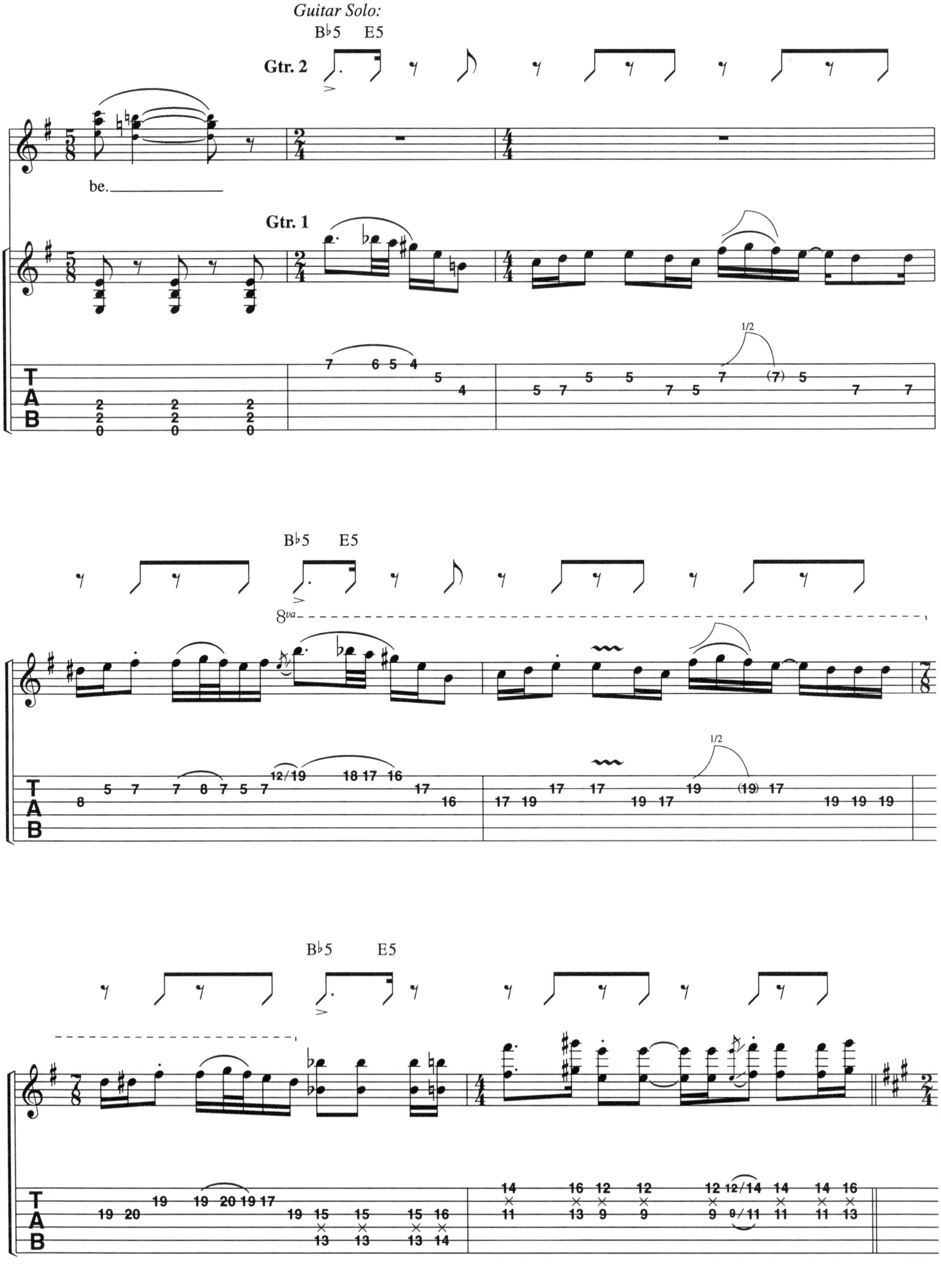
Guitar Solo:
B♭5 E5
Gtr. 2
be.
Gtr. 1
1/2
B♭5 E5
8va
1/2
B♭5 E5

E
Leave me a- lone
leave me a-
Gtr. 1 w/distant reverb
poco dim.
let ring
hold bend
let ring
D
A
lone,
leave
me
E
D
a - lone.
I just want to be a -
let ring
let ring

Verse:
w/Rhy. Fig. 2 (Gtr. 2, 4 1/2 times) simile
E
lone. 4. Don't feel sor-ry it's not your con-cern. On-ly the
Gtr. 2
let ring
T
A
B
D Asus A E
lone-ly are the ones who get burned. Safe in my nest my home
D
sweet home, No in-vit-ed guests, I just want,
Outro Chorus:
Asus A E
I just want, I just wan-na be a-lone.
Bkgd. vcl: I wish you would leave me a-lone,
D Asus A
Leave me a-lone, leave me a-lone.
I wish you would leave me a-lone.
E/B bass E/A bass
Wish you would leave me a-lone, I wish you would leave me.
I just
Band tacet
N.C.
want to be a-lone.

midnight express

Words and Music by
NUNO BETTENCOURT/GARY CHERONE

*Tune as follows:
- ⑥ = C ③ = F
- ⑤ = G ② = A
- ④ = C ① = C

*"Dropped D" tuning down one whole step.

Midnight Express - 9 - 1
PG9515

Copyright © 1995 COLOR ME BLIND MUSIC (ASCAP)
All Rights Administered by ALMO MUSIC CORP. (ASCAP) Throughout the World Under License from FUNKY METAL MUSIC, INC.
International Copyright Secured   Made in U.S.A.   All Rights Reserved

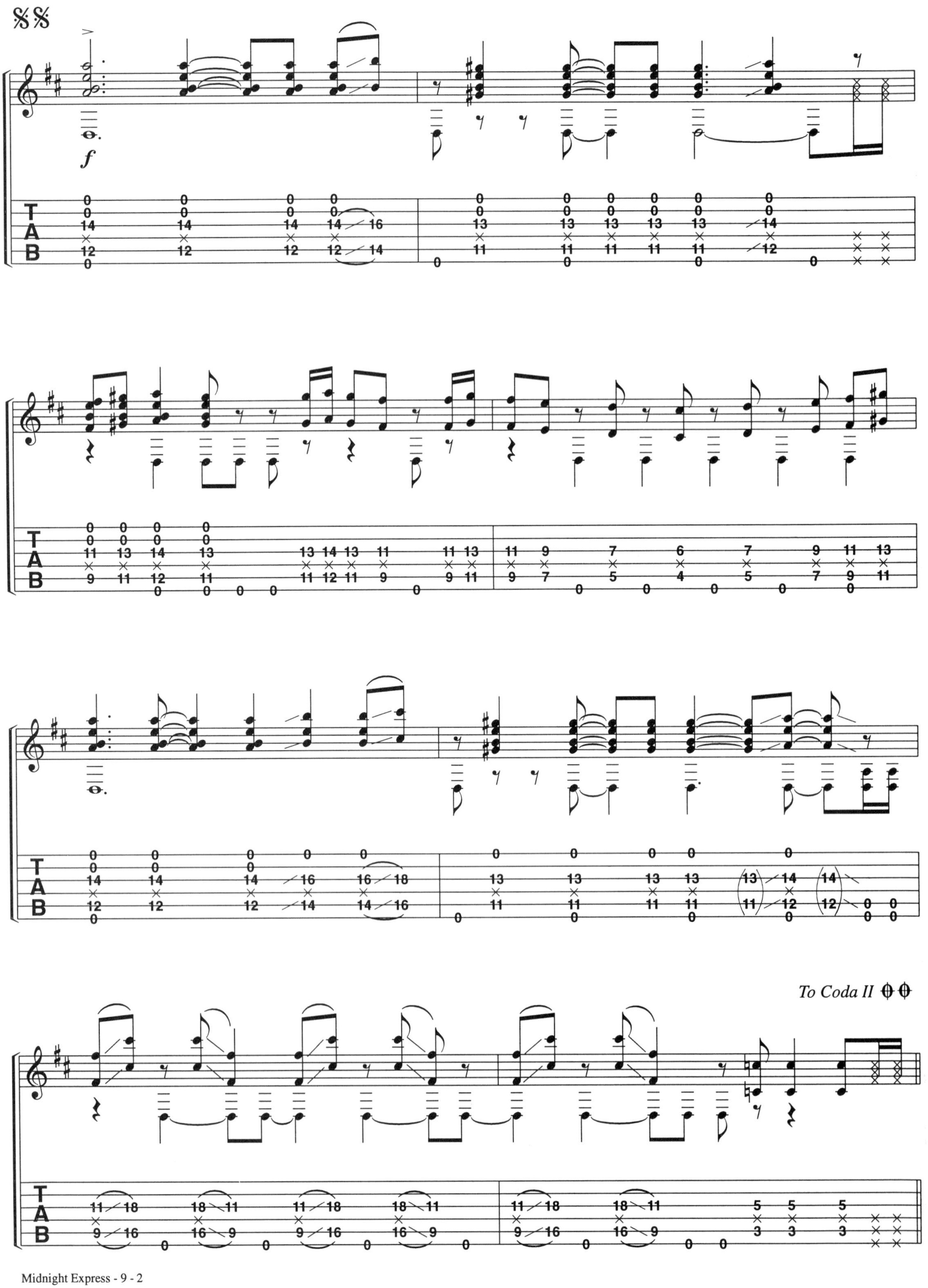
To Coda II

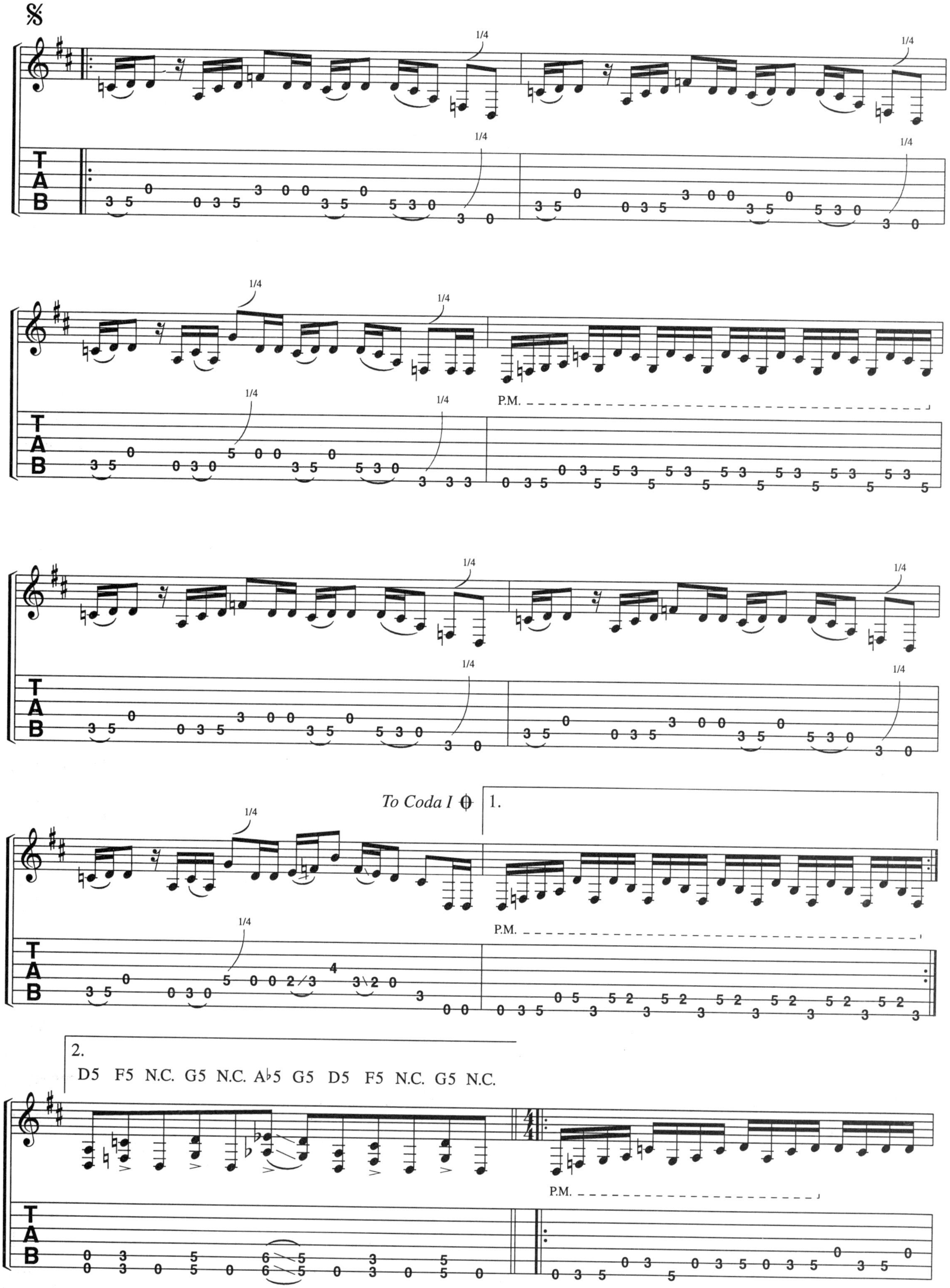
To Coda I
1.
2.
D5 F5 N.C. G5 N.C. A♭5 G5 D5 F5 N.C. G5 N.C.
P.M.
1/4

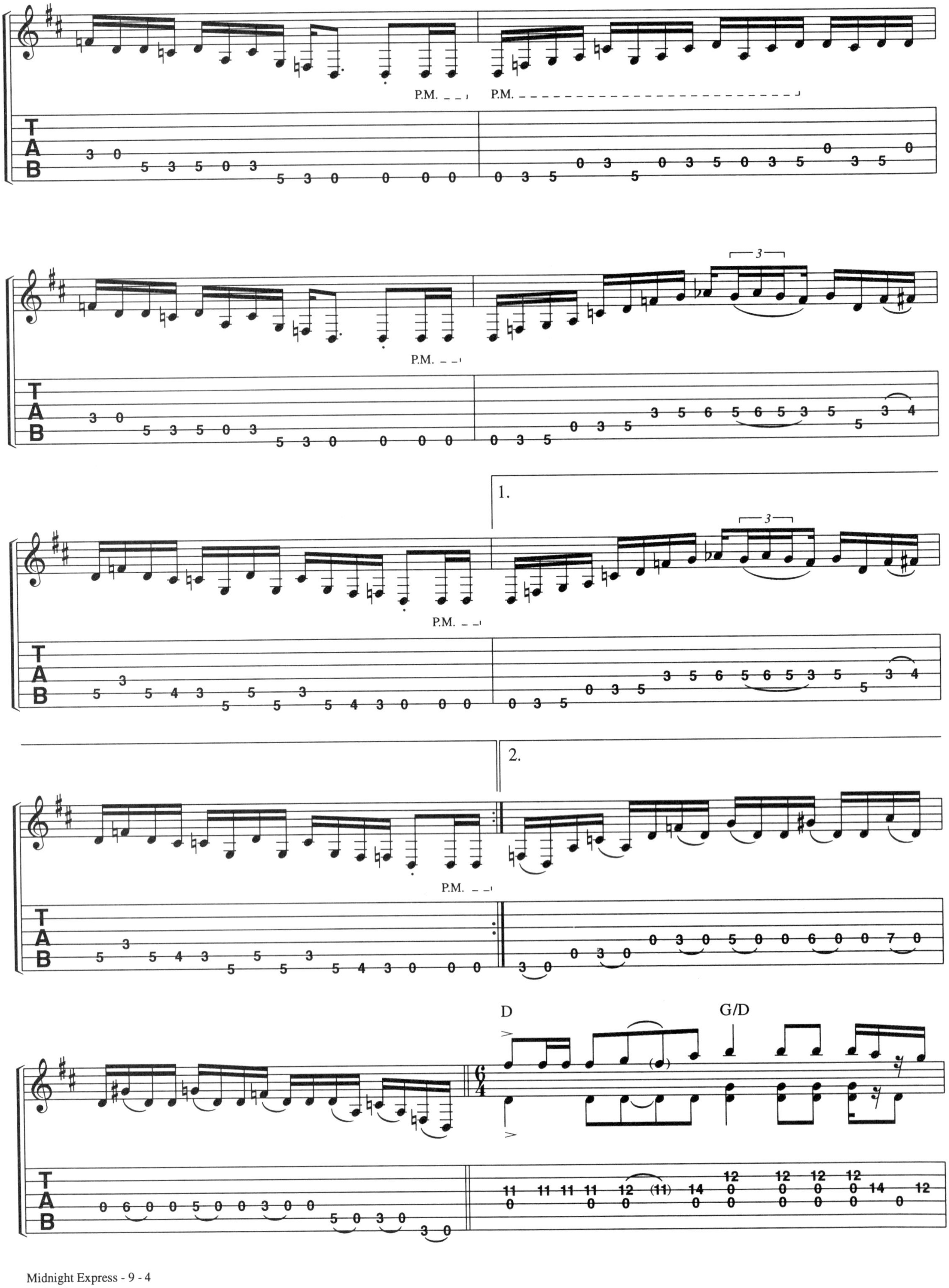
P.M.
P.M.
P.M.
1.
P.M.
2.
P.M.
D
G/D

D
Gm/D
D
A7/D
TAB
D
G/D
TAB
D
Gm/D
D
A7/D
TAB
N.C.
P.M.
P.M.
P.M.
P.M.
P.M.
TAB
A7
A7sus
N.C.
P.M.
P.M.
P.M.
P.M.
P.M.
P.M.
P.M.
P.M.
TAB

A7
A7sus
N.C.
P.M.
A7 A7sus
N.C.
P.M.
A7
A7sus
B♭6(♯11)
let ring
C
let ring
D
G/D
D
Gm/D
D
A7
A7/D
TAB

D
G/D
TAB
D
Gm/D
D
A7/D
TAB
N.C.
P.M.
P.M.
P.M.
P.M.
TAB
A7
A7sus
N.C.
P.M.
P.M.
P.M.
P.M.
P.M.
P.M.
P.M.
P.M.
TAB
A7
Gm/A
N.C.
P.M.
P.M.
P.M.
P.M.
P.M.
TAB

P.M.
P.M.
P.M.
P.M.
P.M.
G
B♭6(♯11)
C
let ring
let ring
D(4 9)
C
let ring
B♭6
C
D.S. 𝄋 al Coda I
N.C.
P.M.
Coda I
D5 F5 N.C. G5 N.C. G♯5 N.C. A5 N.C. B♭5 N.C.
D.S.S. 𝄋 al Coda II
Coda II
N.C.
P.M.

67

Midnight Express - 9 - 9
PG9515

naked

Words and Music by
NUNO BETTENCOURT/GARY CHERONE/PATRICK BADGER

Tune down 1/2 step:
- ⑥ = E♭   ③ = G♭
- ⑤ = A♭   ② = B♭
- ④ = D♭   ① = E♭

Chords: D7 (10fr.), D7sus (10fr.), D♭7 (9fr.)

Slowly ♩ = 64

Intro:

Lyrics: 1. So you want__ me__ to take__ it off,__

Naked - 13 - 1
PG9515

Copyright © 1995 COLOR ME BLIND MUSIC and PASTY FACE MUSIC (ASCAP)
All Rights Administered by ALMO MUSIC CORP. (ASCAP) Throughout the World Under License from FUNKY METAL MUSIC, INC.
International Copyright Secured   Made in U.S.A.   All Rights Reserved

E5 N.C. A N.C.
just to see what's un-der-neath my cloth. I'll
hold hold
T A B
A N.C.
show you I'm ev-'ry inch a man. Meas-ure
harm.
hold
harm.
A N.C.
all that you think you can.
(vib. w/bar) trem. bar
hold
f
1/2

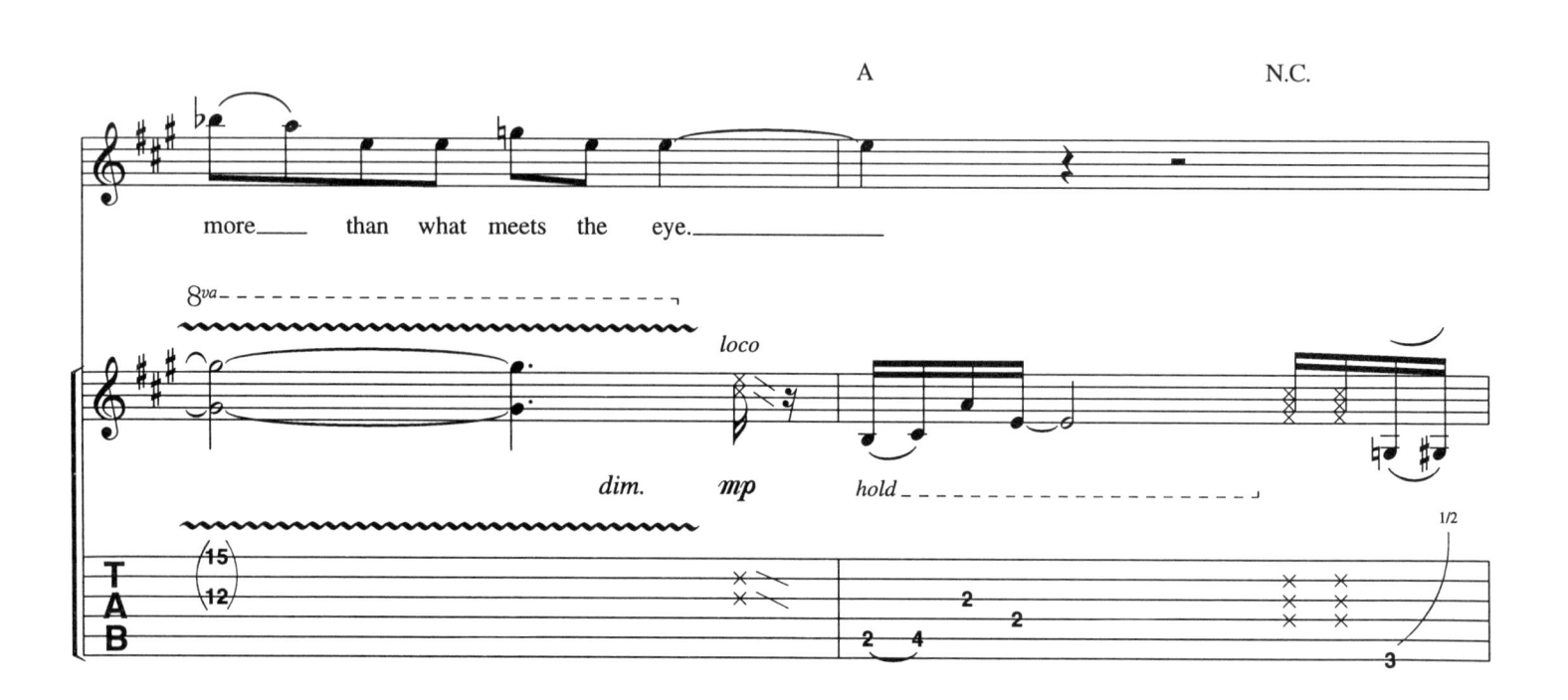

Riff A

8va ... end Riff A, loco

2. Be - cause__ I'm more__ than what meets the eye.__

(vib. w/bar)

8va ... loco

dim. **mp** *hold*

Naked - 13 - 3
PG9515

E5
N.C.
Flesh 'n' blood is of - ten a white lie.
By the
1/2
1
co- ver you mis - judge the book.
I said,
A.H.
15ma
A.H.
1
1
1
Pitch: D E D
E5
N.C.
"O- pen your mind and take an- oth- er, o- pen your mind and take an- oth- er look!"
f
1/2
1

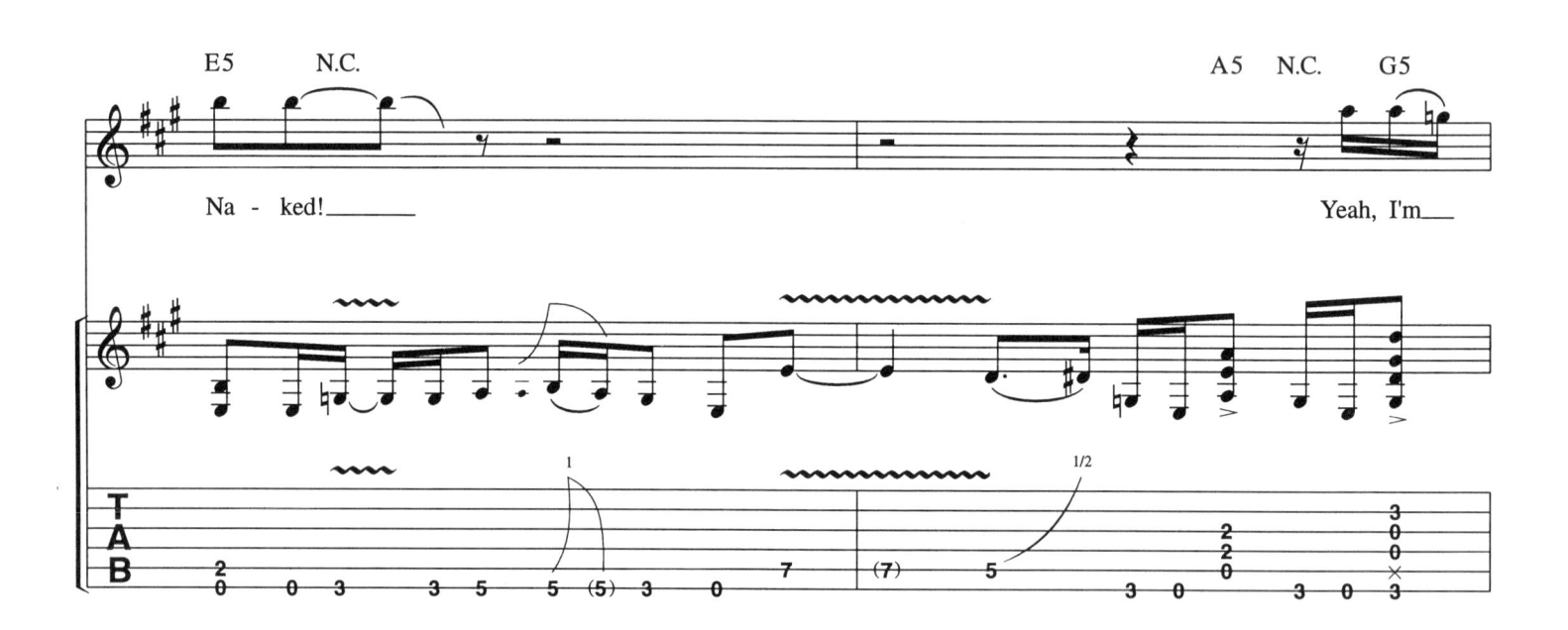

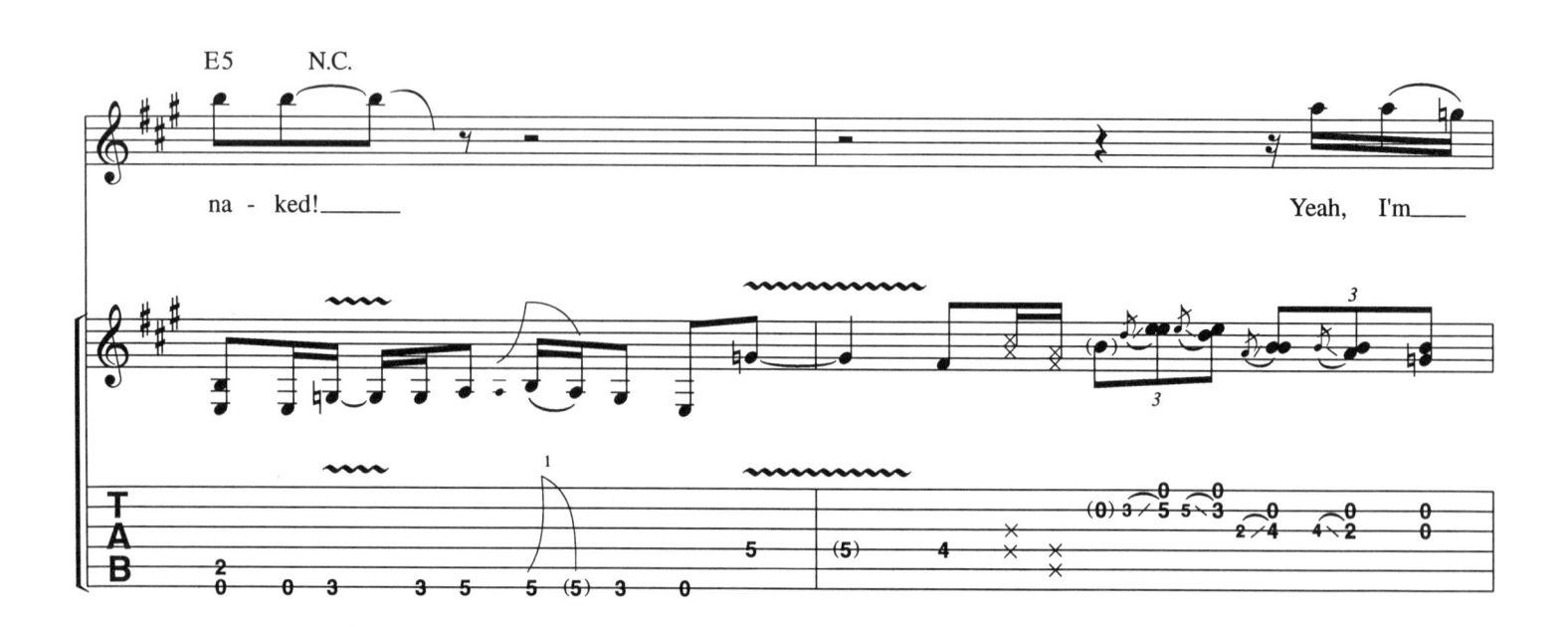

Chorus:
w/Riff A (2 times)

Na - ked and I'm un - a - shamed. Na - ked, with no one to blame.

Yeah, you want the truth? Na - ked, here's my birth - day suit.

Na - ked! Yeah, I'm

na - ked! Yeah, I'm

73

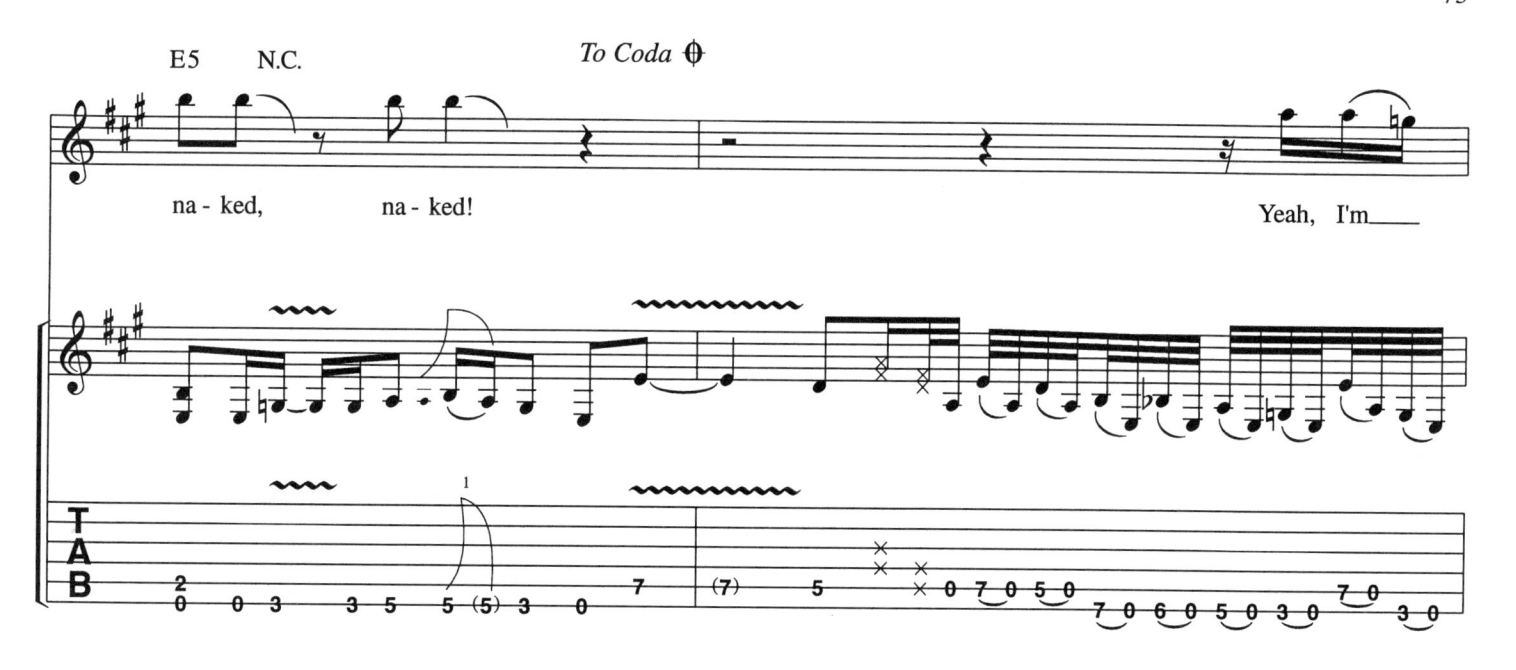

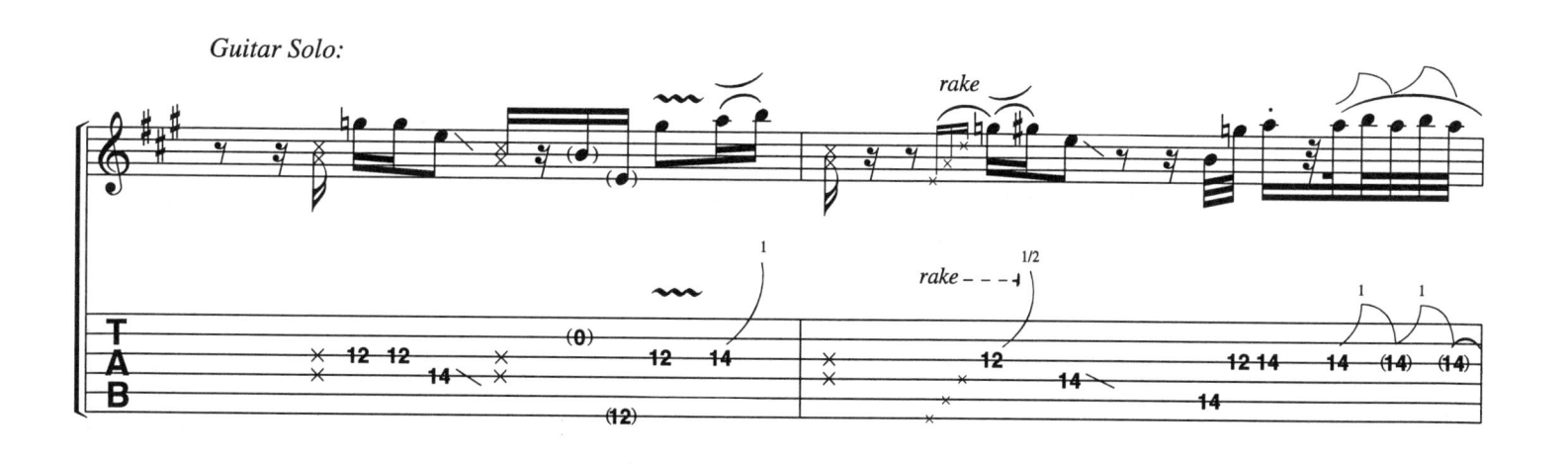

Guitar Solo:

Naked - 13 - 6
PG9515

Verse 3:

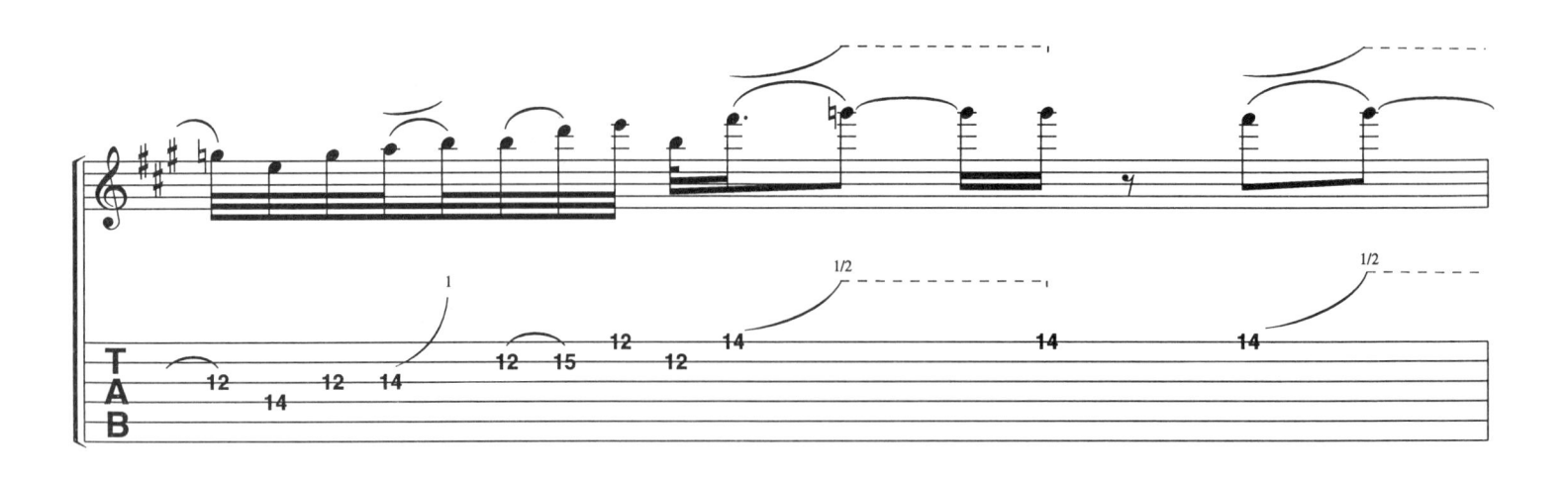

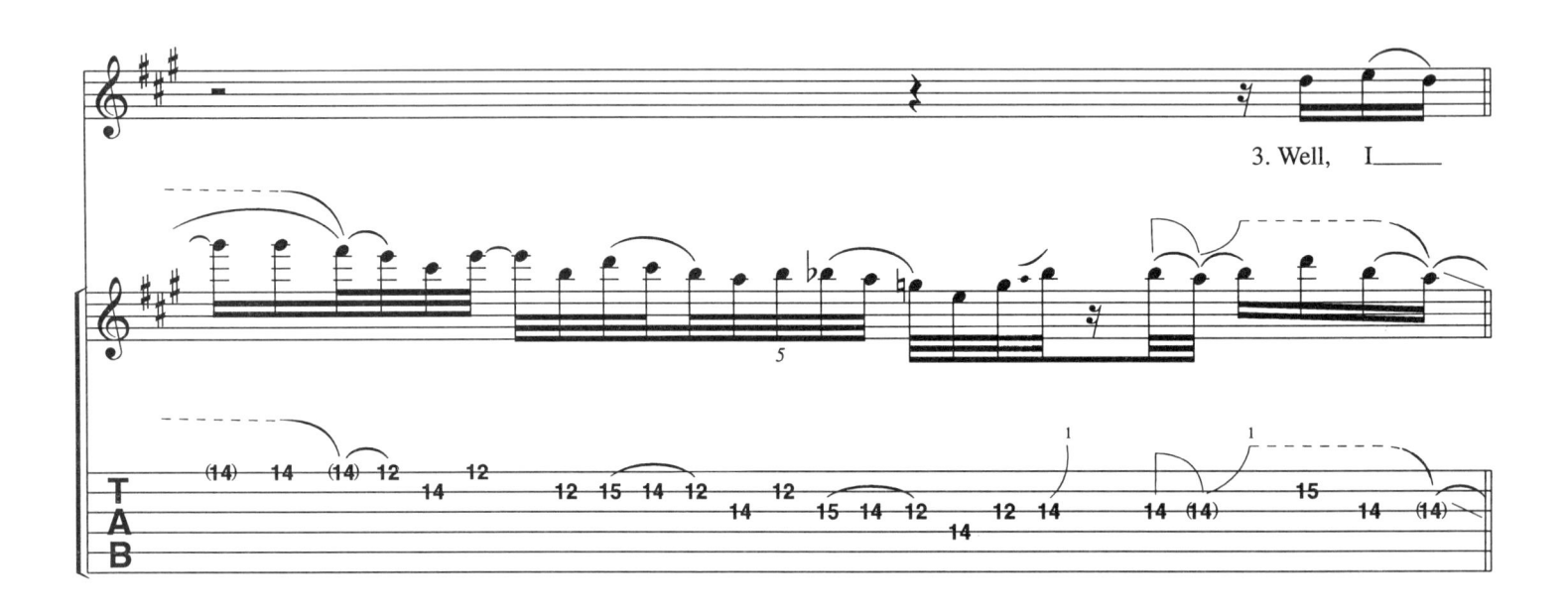

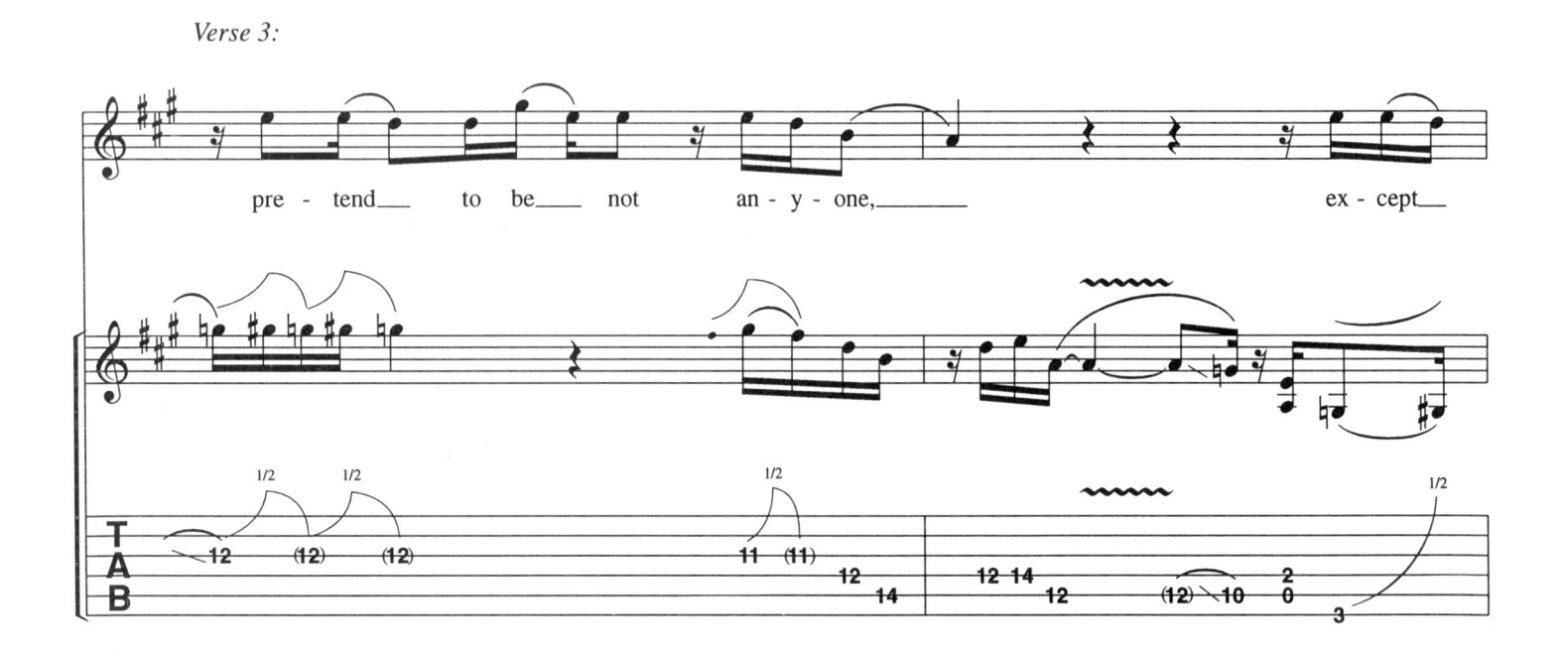

3. Well, I pre - tend to be not an - y - one, ex - cept

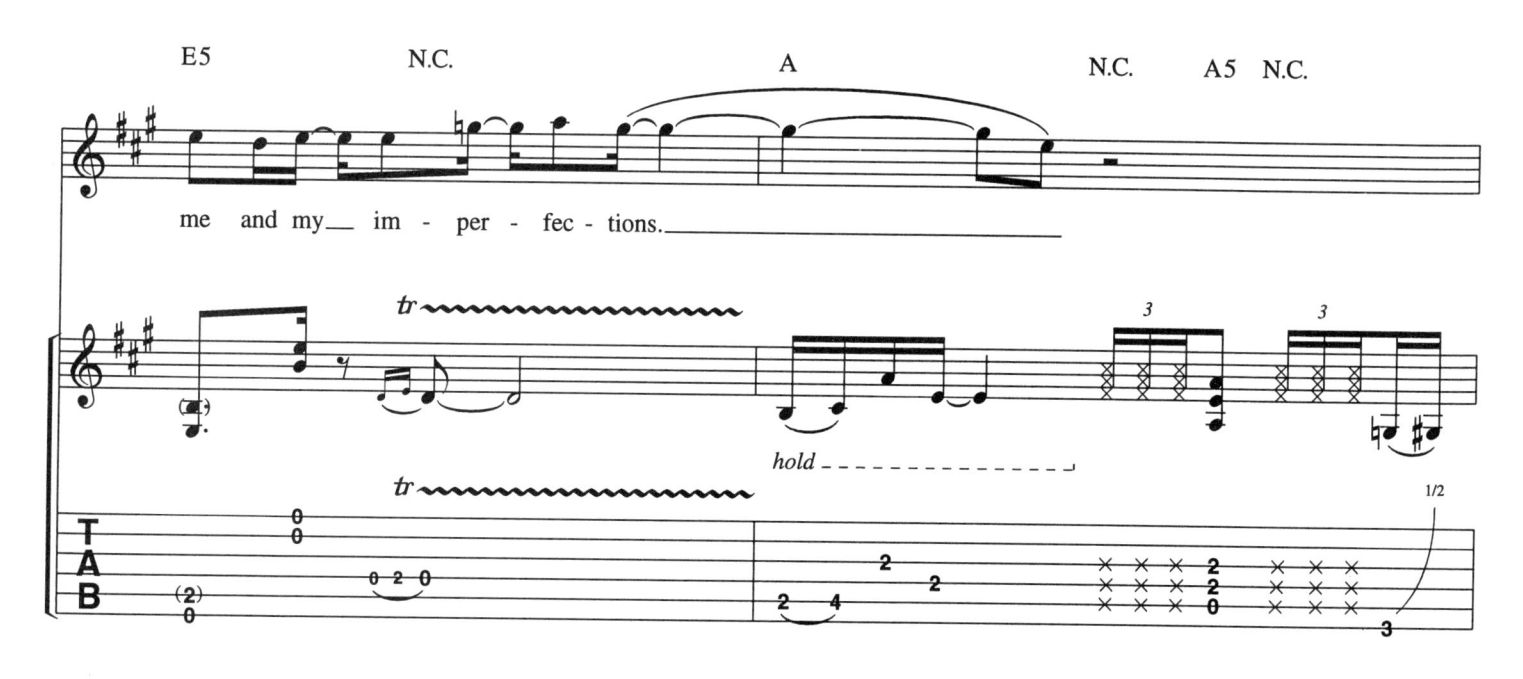

me and my_ im - per - fec - tions._

There is no - thing I ex - pect of you_____ that_

you_ would-n't ex - pect_ of me..._ Yeah, you would-n't ex - pect_ of me,_ too.

Coda

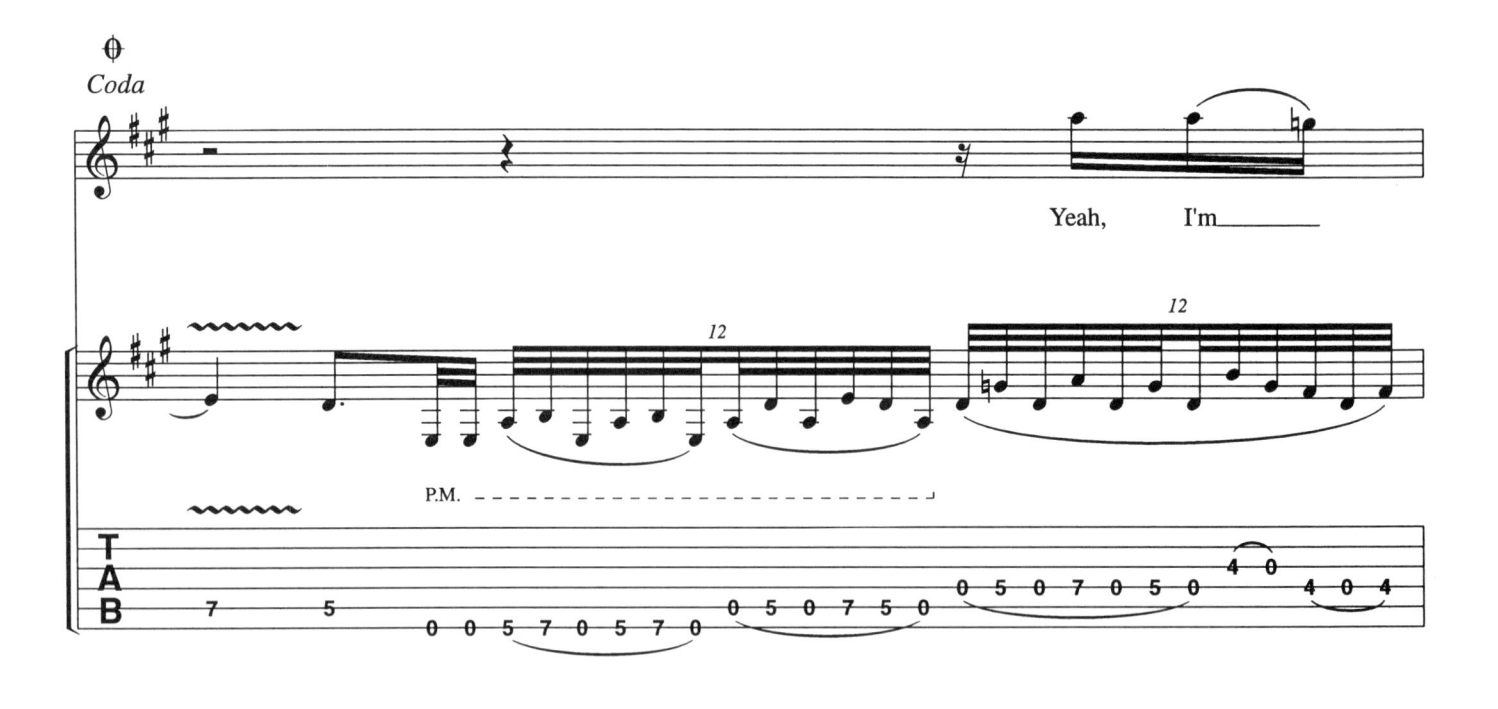

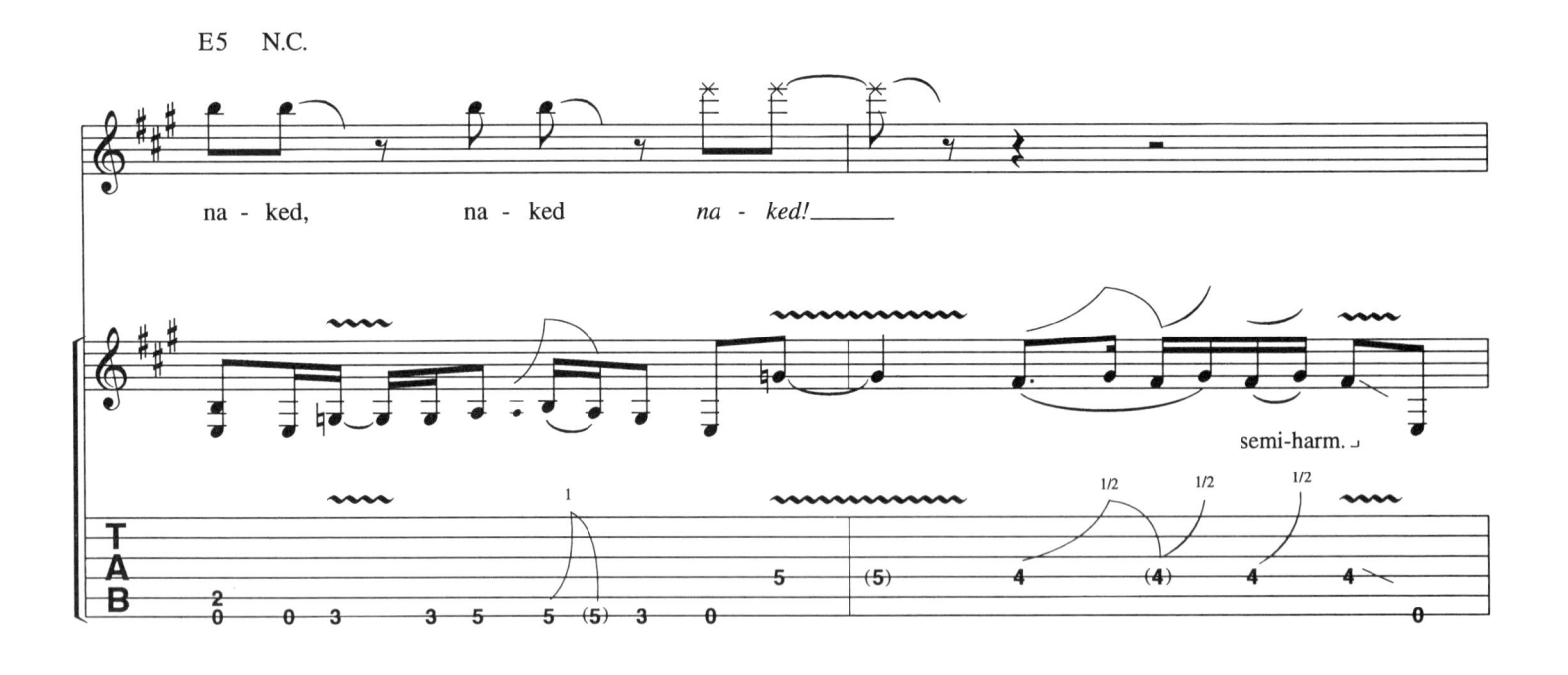

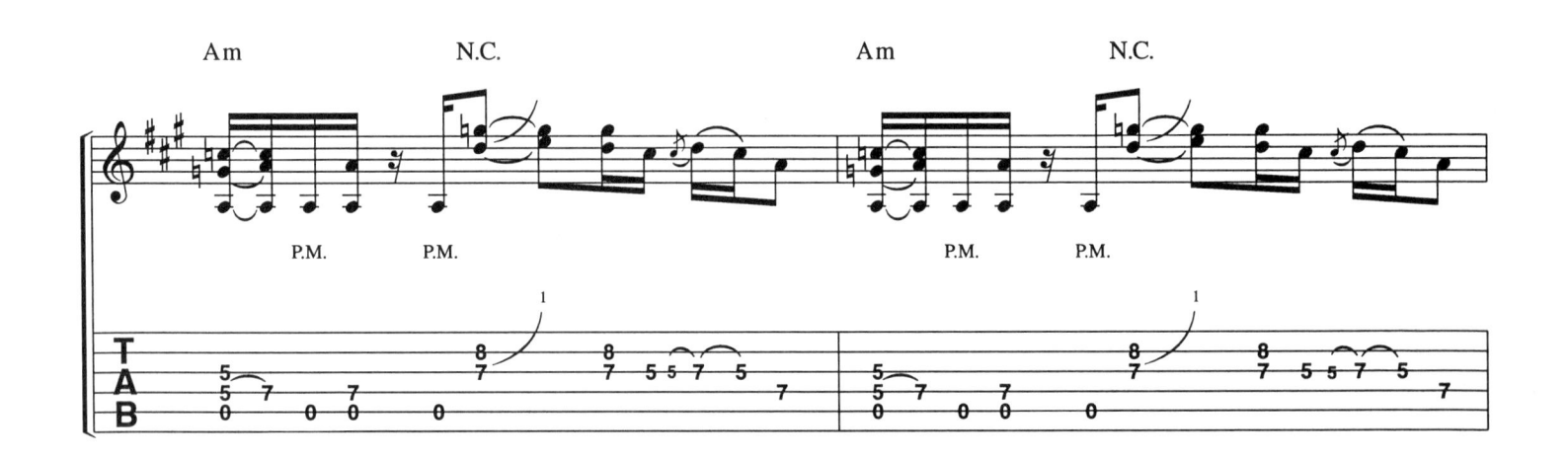

Yeah, I'm na-ked, na-ked na-ked!

Verse 4:

4. Will you excuse me for my ignorance, 'cause I can see only one difference. Well, those of you who seek to find while all the others choose to walk 'n' talk blind!

trem. bar

78

Guitar Solo:

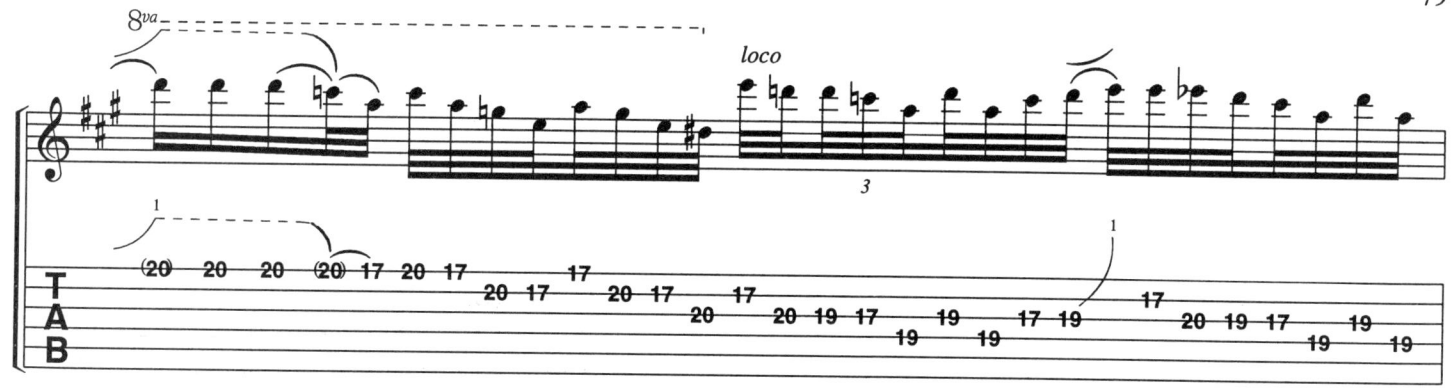

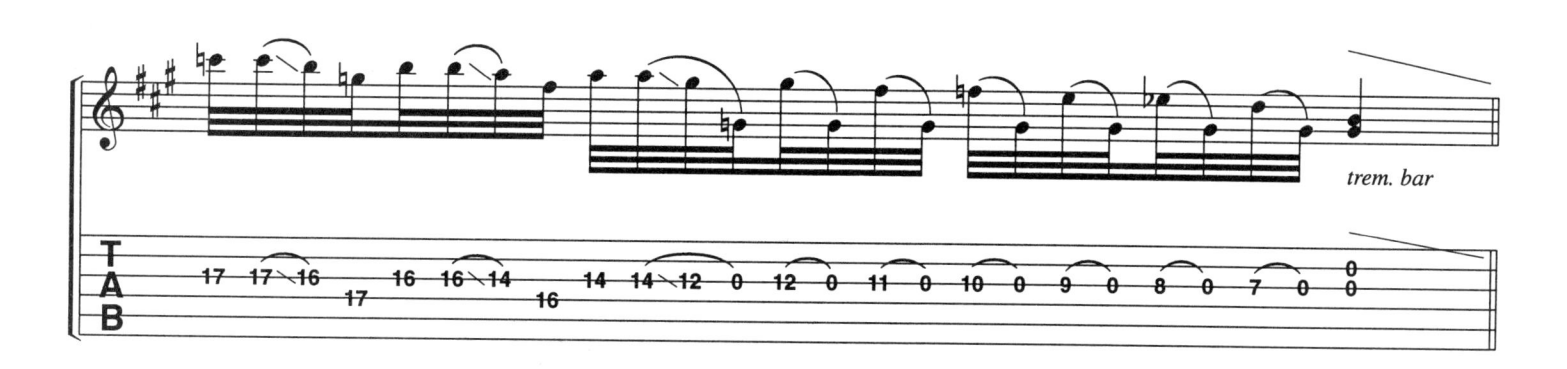

Chorus:

Na - ked! Yeah, I'm

na - ked! Yeah, I'm

Naked - 13 - 12
PG9515

80

no respect

Words and Music by
NUNO BETTENCOURT/GARY CHERONE

All gtrs. tune down 1/2 step:
⑥ = E♭   ③ = G♭
⑤ = A♭   ② = B♭
④ = D♭   ① = E♭

Moderately fast ♩ = 128

*Bass gtr. arranged for gtr.

No Respect - 9 - 1
PG9515

Copyright © 1995 COLOR ME BLIND MUSIC (ASCAP)
All Rights Administered by ALMO MUSIC CORP. (ASCAP) Throughout the World Under License from FUNKY METAL MUSIC, INC.
International Copyright Secured   Made in U.S.A.   All Rights Reserved

you're gonna get it from?

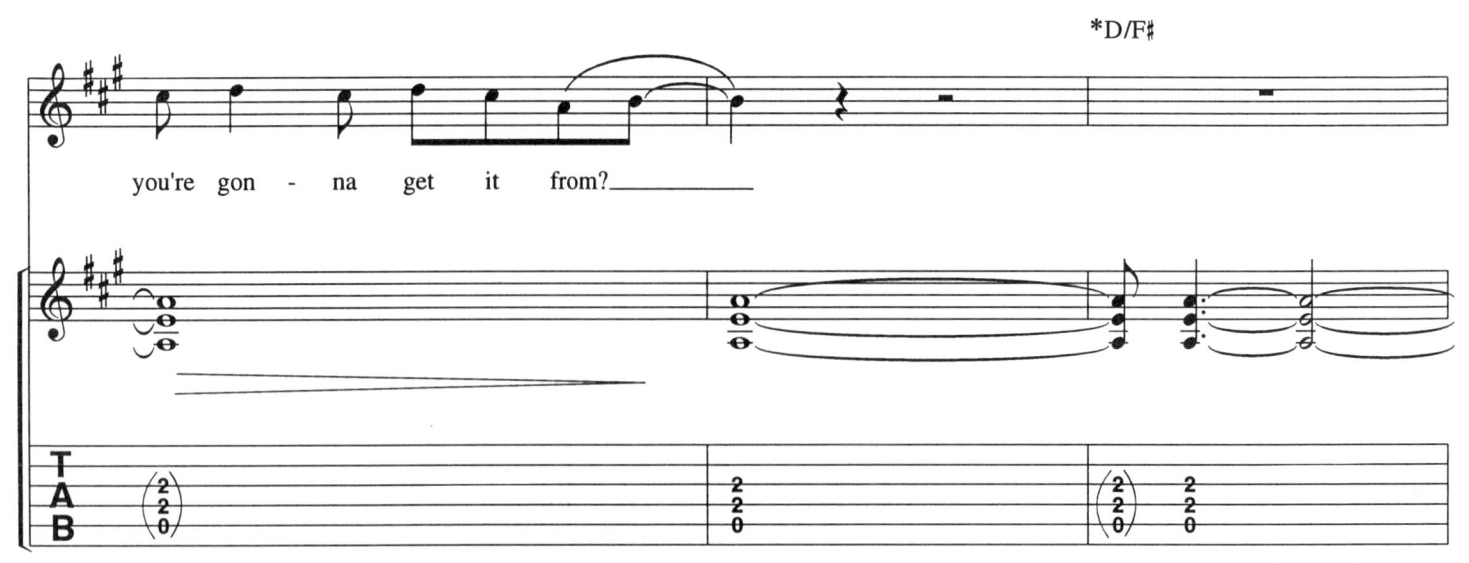

D/F#

*Harmony implied by bass figure.

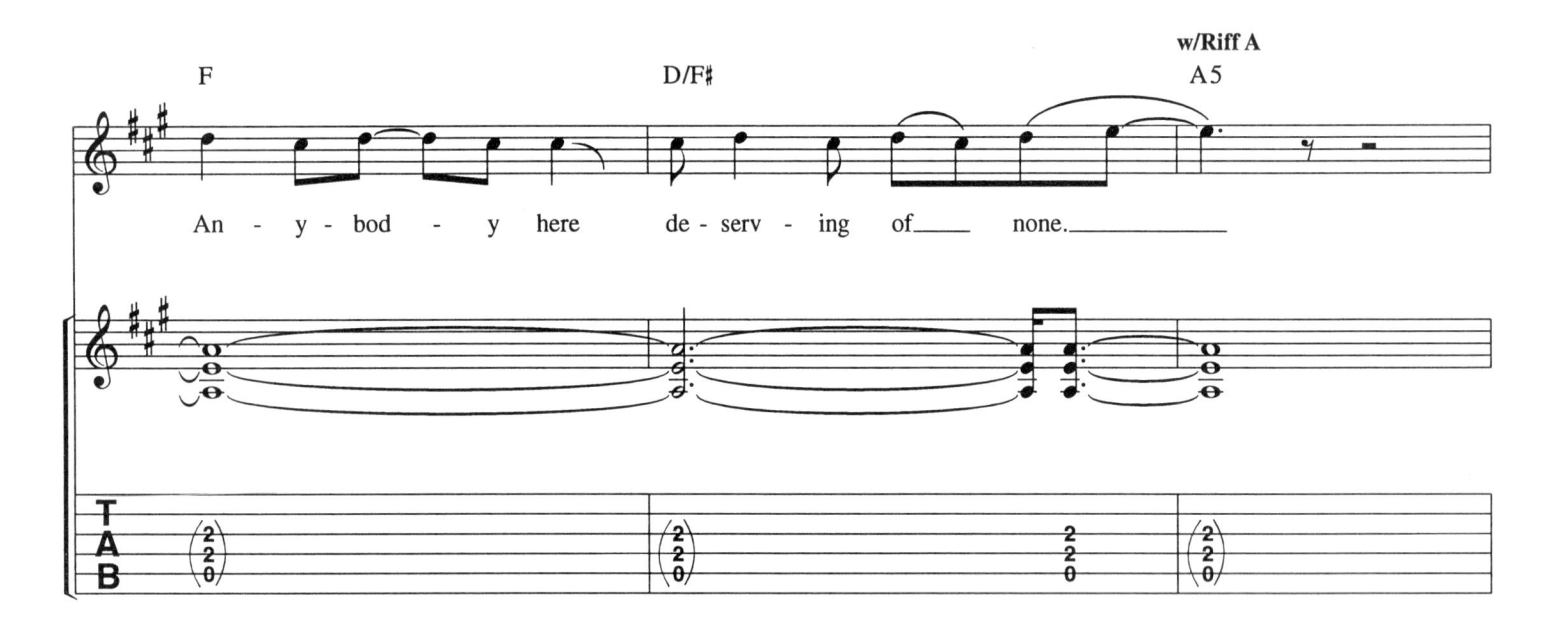

F D/F# A5 w/Riff A

Any-bod-y here de-serv-ing of none.

D/F# F D/F#

So tell me, what makes you think you're not the one.

Gtr. 2 w/dist.

divisi   pick scrape

No Respect - 9 - 2
PG9515

Chorus:
w/Rhy. Fig. 1 *(Gtr. 2 on 2nd verse, simile on repeat)*

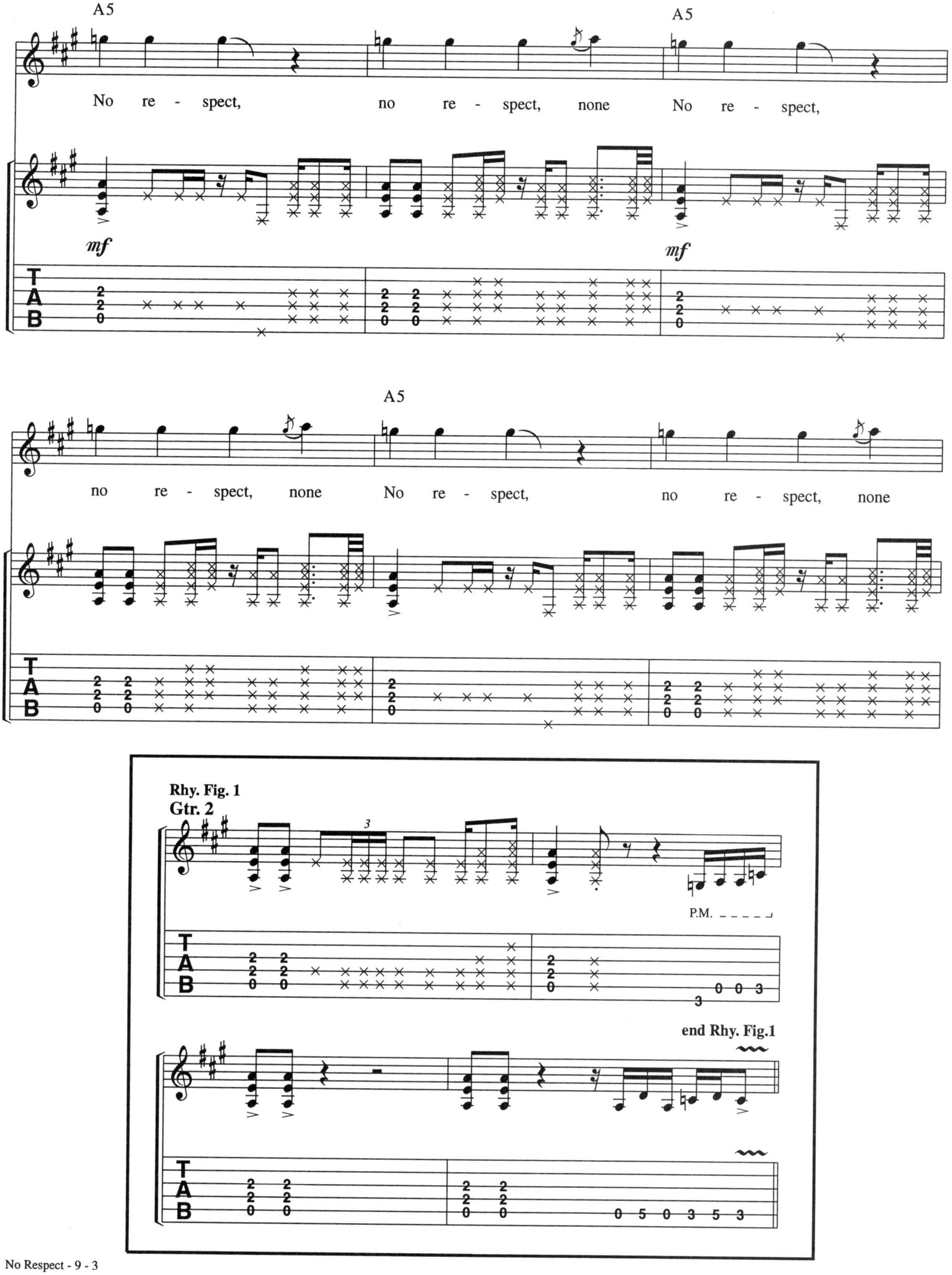

No re - spect, no re - spect, none.

1.

2.
A5 D G A♭

Guitar Solo:
N.C.
A

No re - spect, none.

2nd time play
divisi
steady gliss.

hold bend

G
8va

No Respect - 9 - 4
PG9515

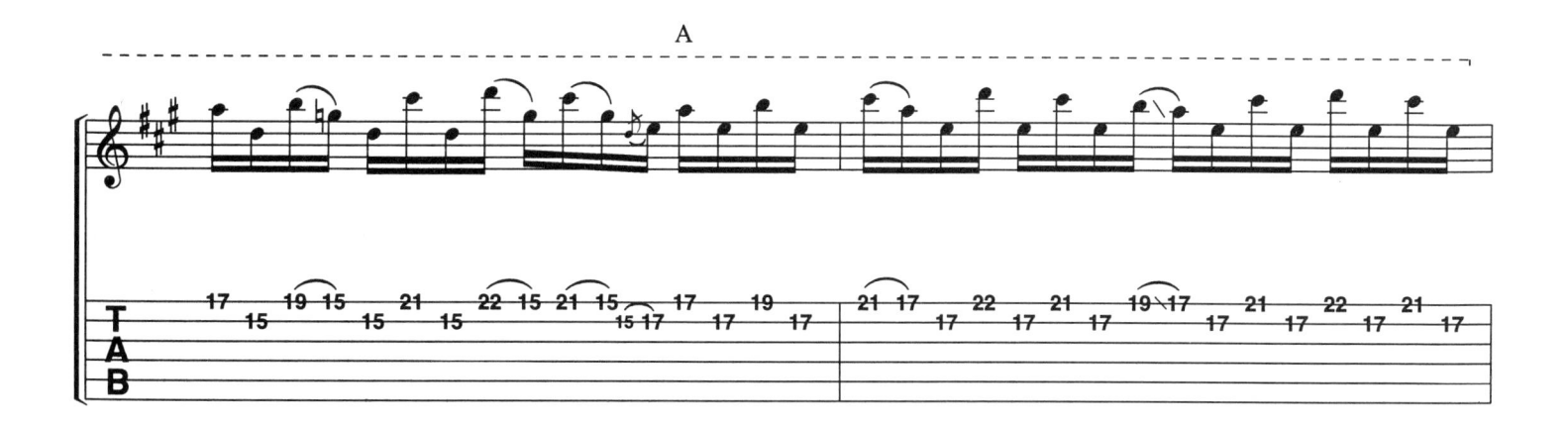

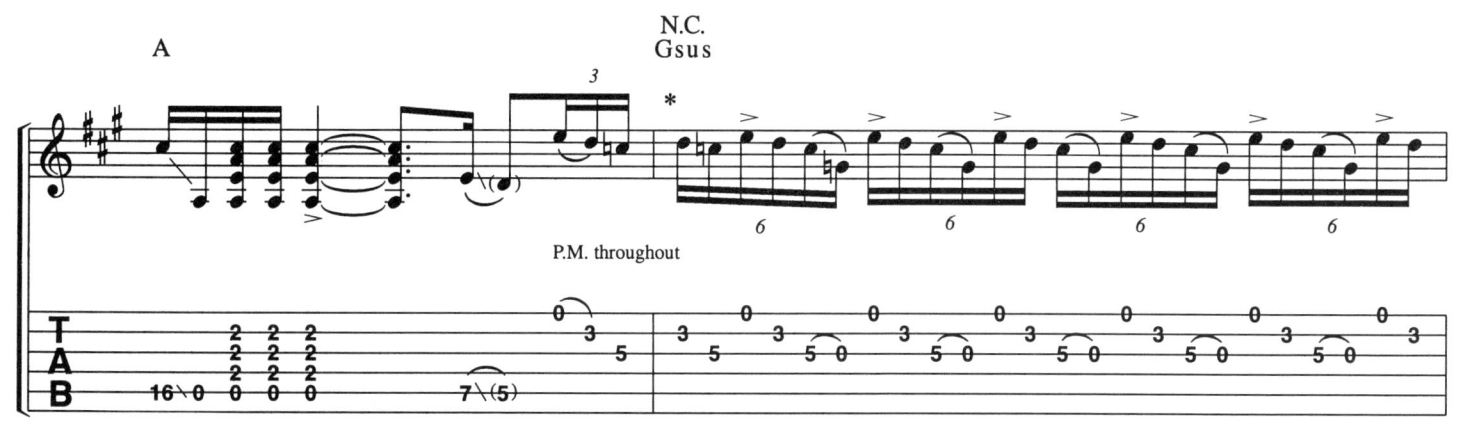

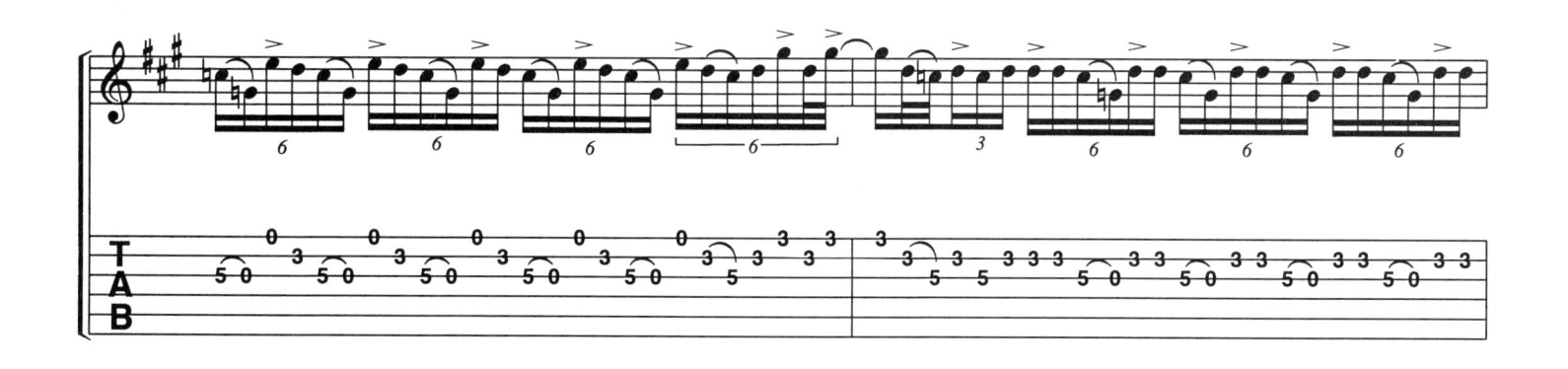

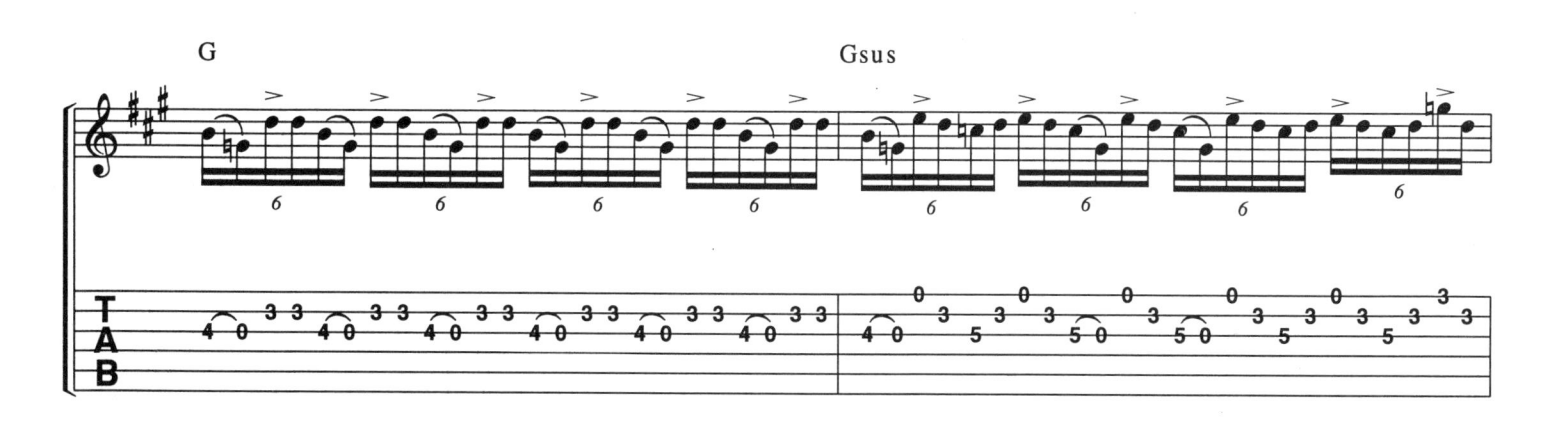

No Respect - 9 - 5
PG9515

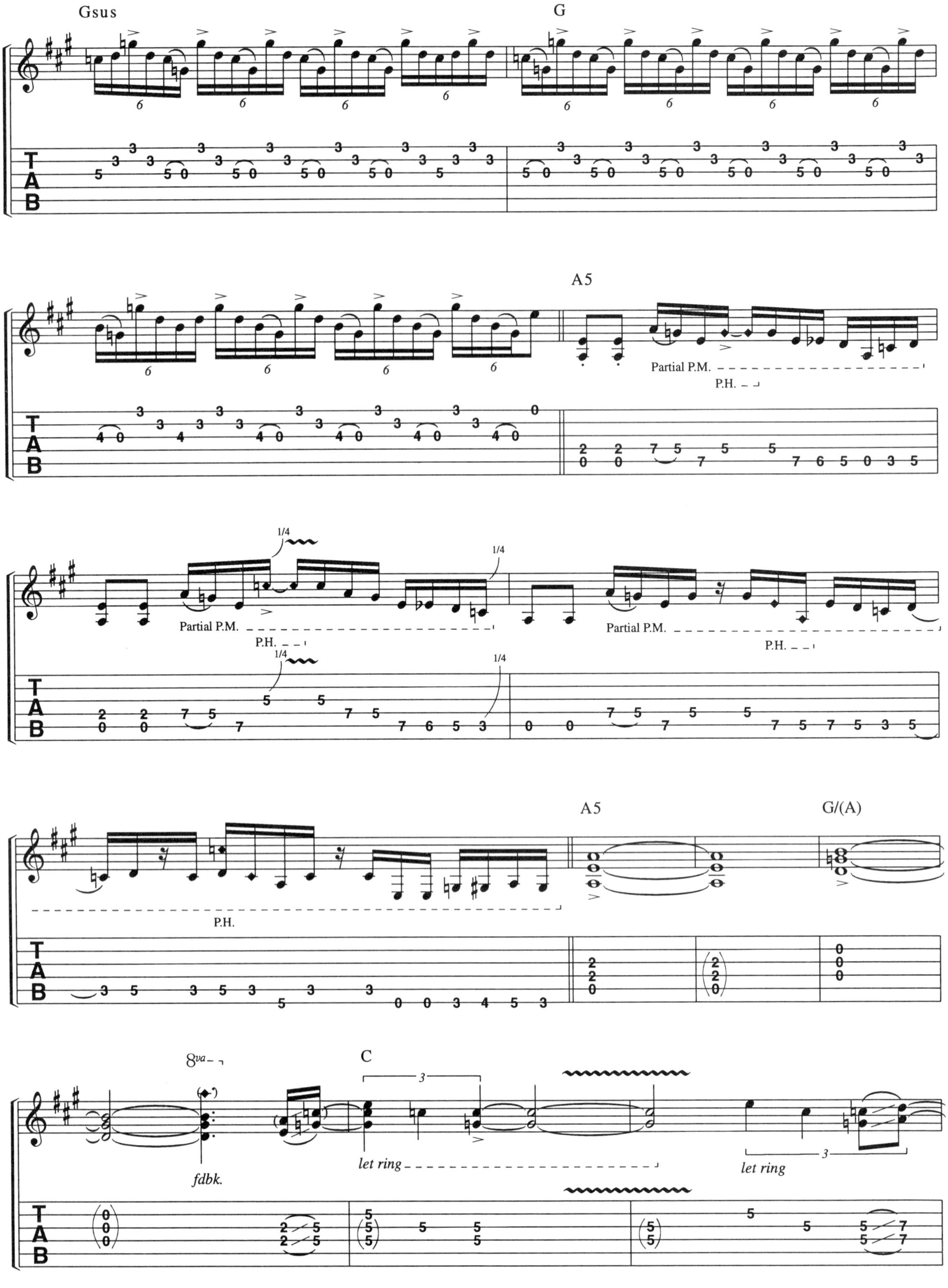
Gsus
G
A5
Partial P.M.
P.H.
1/4
A5
G/(A)
8va
fdbk.
C
let ring
TAB

87

divisi *pick scrape*

Chorus:

A5

No re - spect, no re - spect, none.

A5

No re - spect, no re - spect, none.

A5

No re - spect, no re - spect, none.

No Respect - 9 - 7
PG9515

1.
No re - spect, no re - spect, none.
P.M.
2.
A5
Outro:
w/vcl. ad lib.
B/(A)
No re - spect, none!
C
D
let ring
w/bar
let ring
w/bar
A5
G5/(A)
P.M.

Verse 2:
Respect,
Why be concerned with public adulation.
Respect,
Pat on the back crying for attention.
Respect,
Finding out what it really means to me.
Respect,
Honor comes only after humility.

shadow boxing

Words and Music by
NUNO BETTENCOURT/GARY CHERONE

All gtrs. tune down 1/2 step:
⑥ = E♭ ③ = G♭
⑤ = A♭ ② = B♭
④ = D♭ ① = E♭

Moderately slow rock ♩ = 86
Intro:

Shadow Boxing - 13 - 1
PG9515

Copyright © 1995 COLOR ME BLIND MUSIC (ASCAP)
All Rights Administered by ALMO MUSIC CORP. (ASCAP) Throughout the World Under License from FUNKY METAL MUSIC, INC.
International Copyright Secured   Made in U.S.A.   All Rights Reserved

Verse:
w/Rhy. Fig. 2 *(Gtr. 1) simile*

Dm7

1. Last round, looks like I'm in for a fight. Knocked down, there is nowhere left to hide. Stick 'n' move and

Shadow Boxing - 13 - 2
PG9515

when I try to run a - way,
old one, two,
I
1/4
hold bend
1
T
A
B
G7
on - ly end up face to face.
let ring
Mir - ror, mir - ror,
let ring

it's get - ting clear - er, _____ oh.

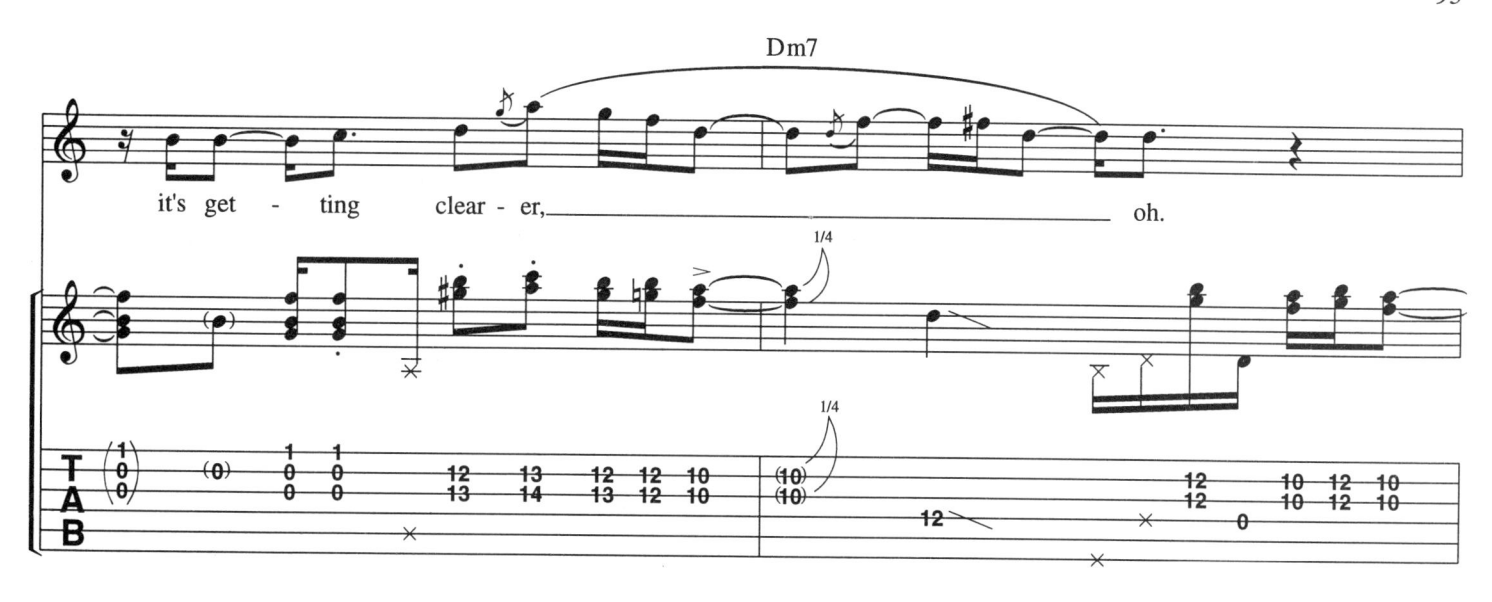

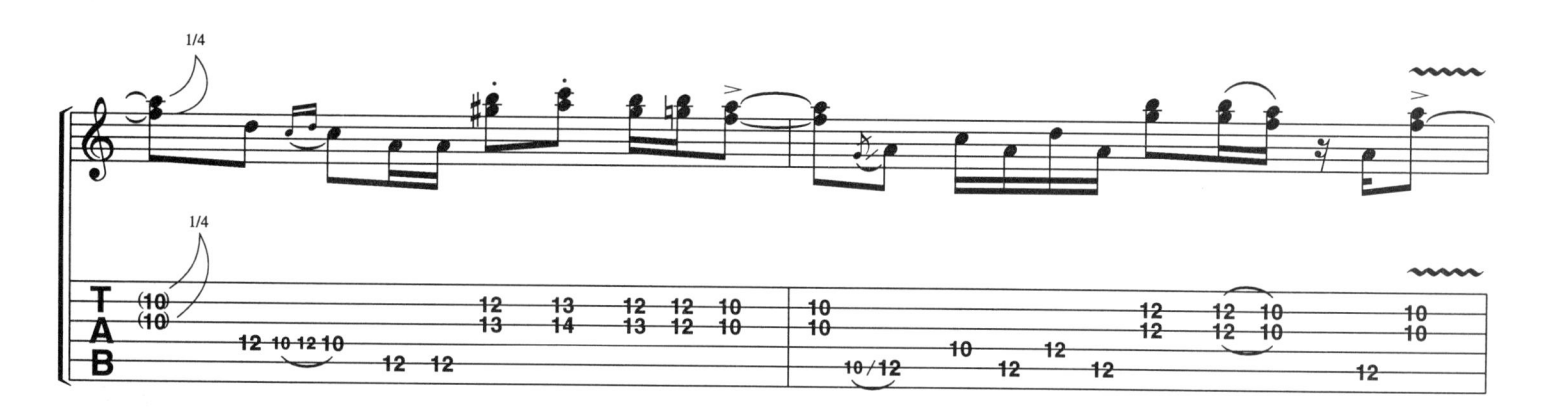

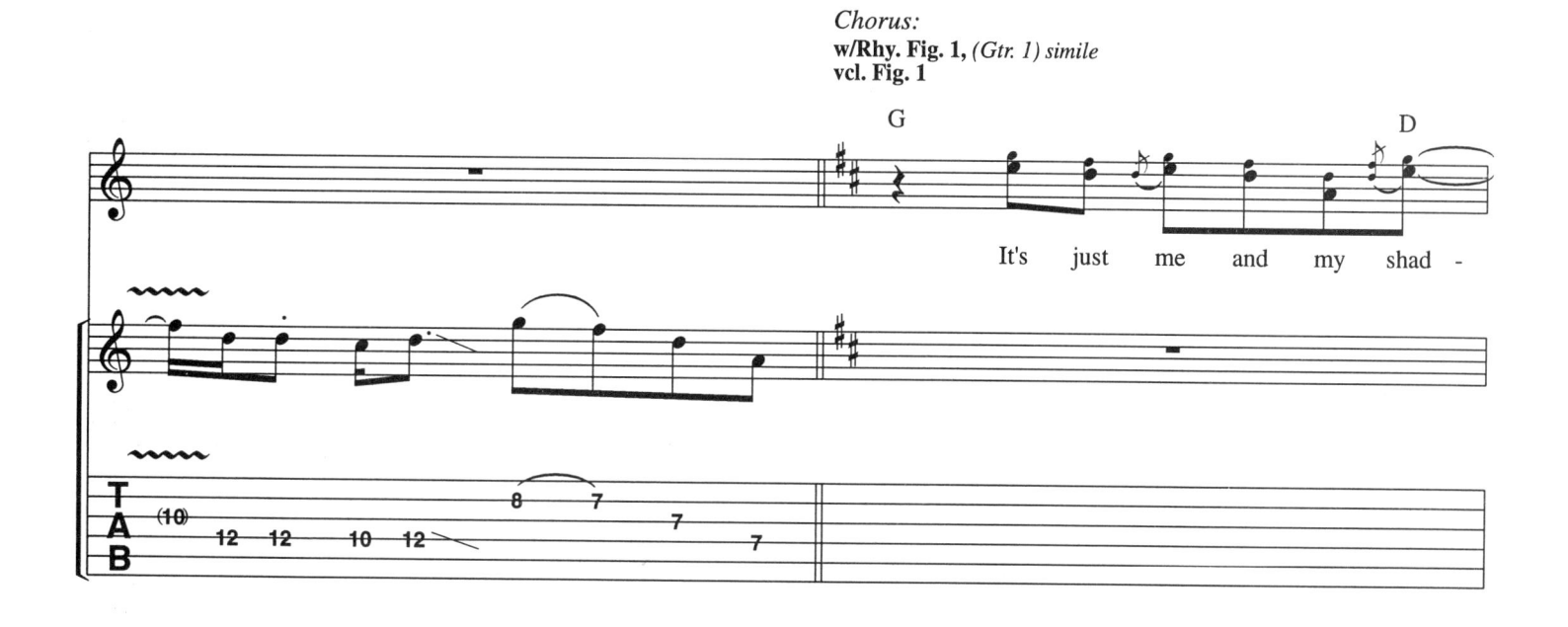

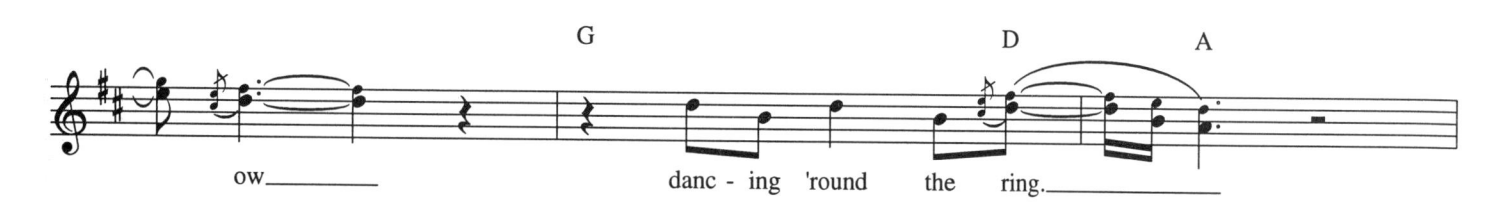

Chorus:
w/Rhy. Fig. 1, (Gtr. 1) simile
vcl. Fig. 1

It's just me and my shad - ow ____ danc - ing 'round the ring.

Lyrics:

I try to fight it, but then how can I win when I'm only shadow boxing.

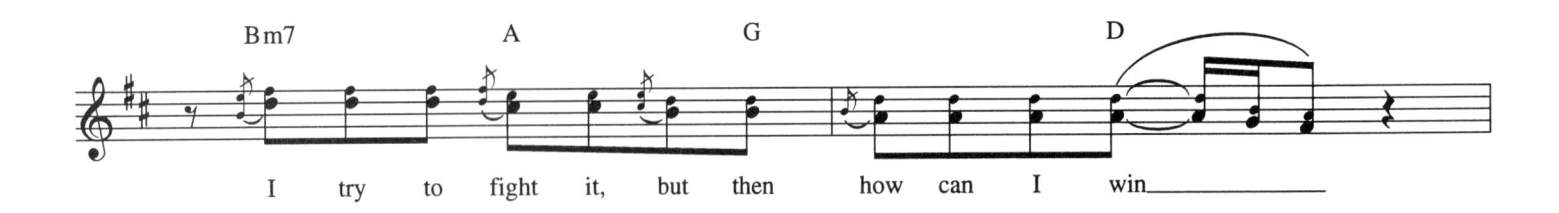

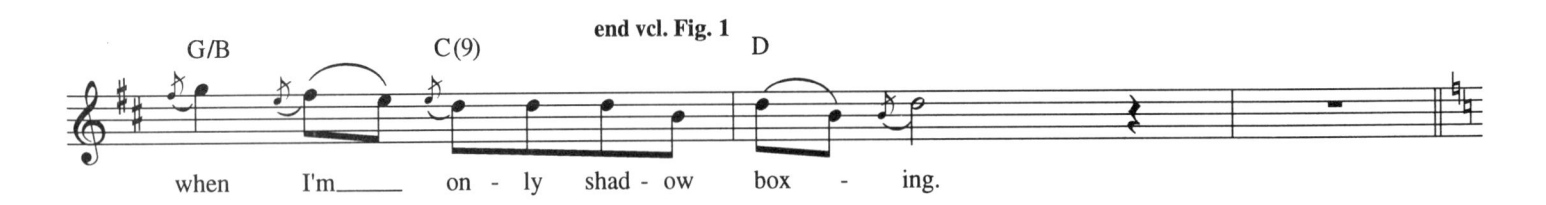

Verse 2:
Time out, I'm looking for a standing eight, no doubt, yeah. My inside has come out to play.

w/wah effect

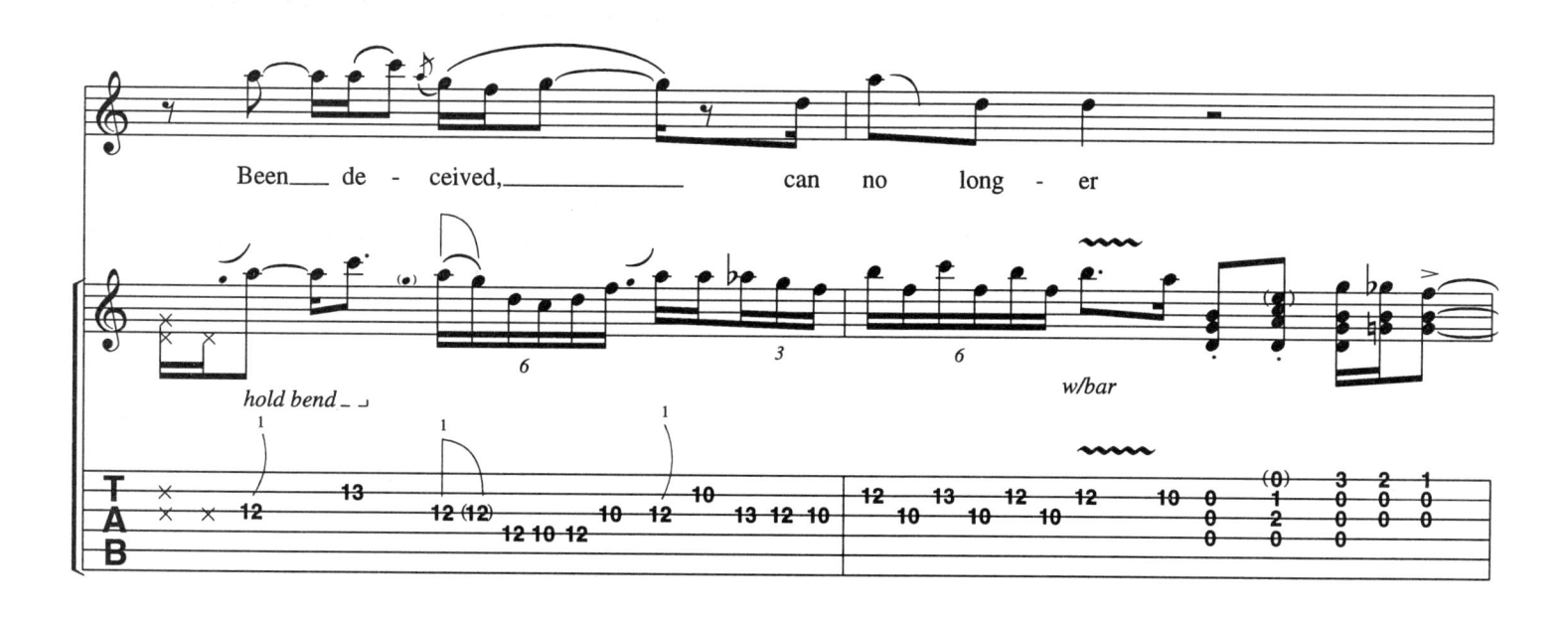

Bob 'n' weave, it's conscious of my ev'ry move.

Been deceived, can no longer

G7

ignore the truth. Mirror, mirror,

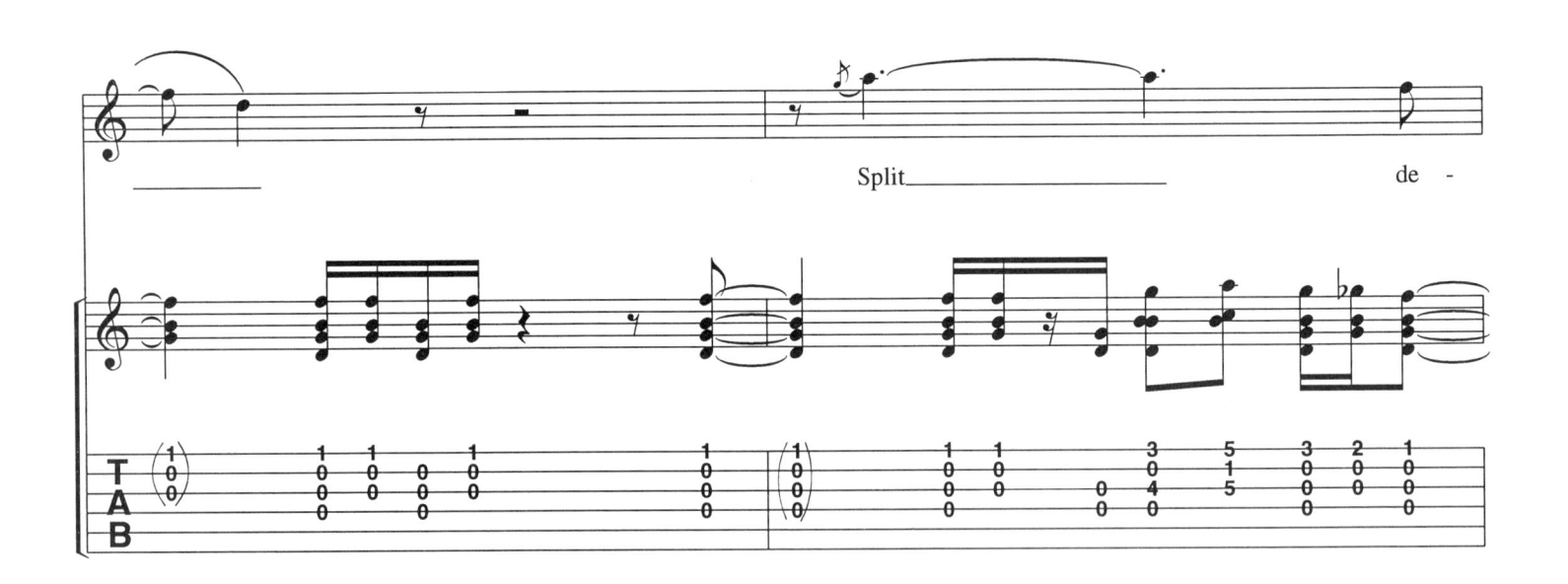

it's get - ting clear - er.

Split_____ de - cis - ion_____ blurs_____ my vis - ion._____

Shadow Boxing - 13 - 7
PG9515

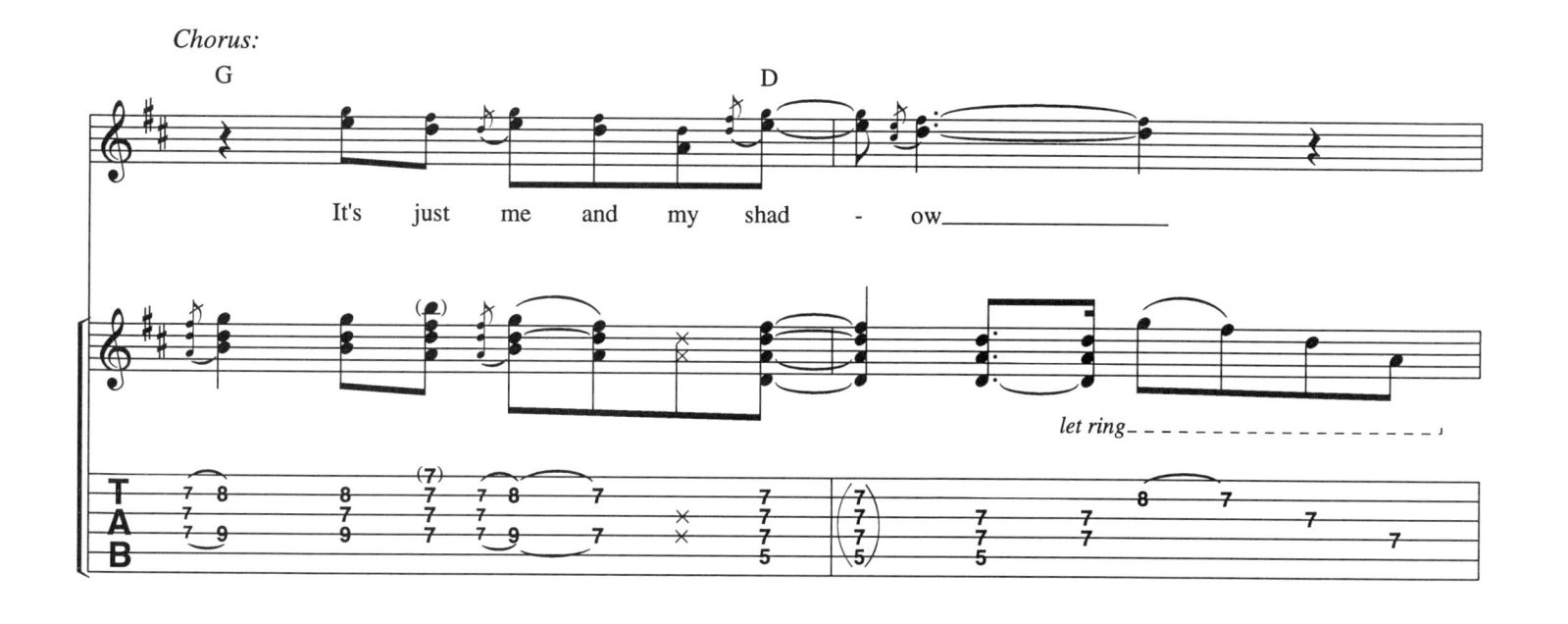

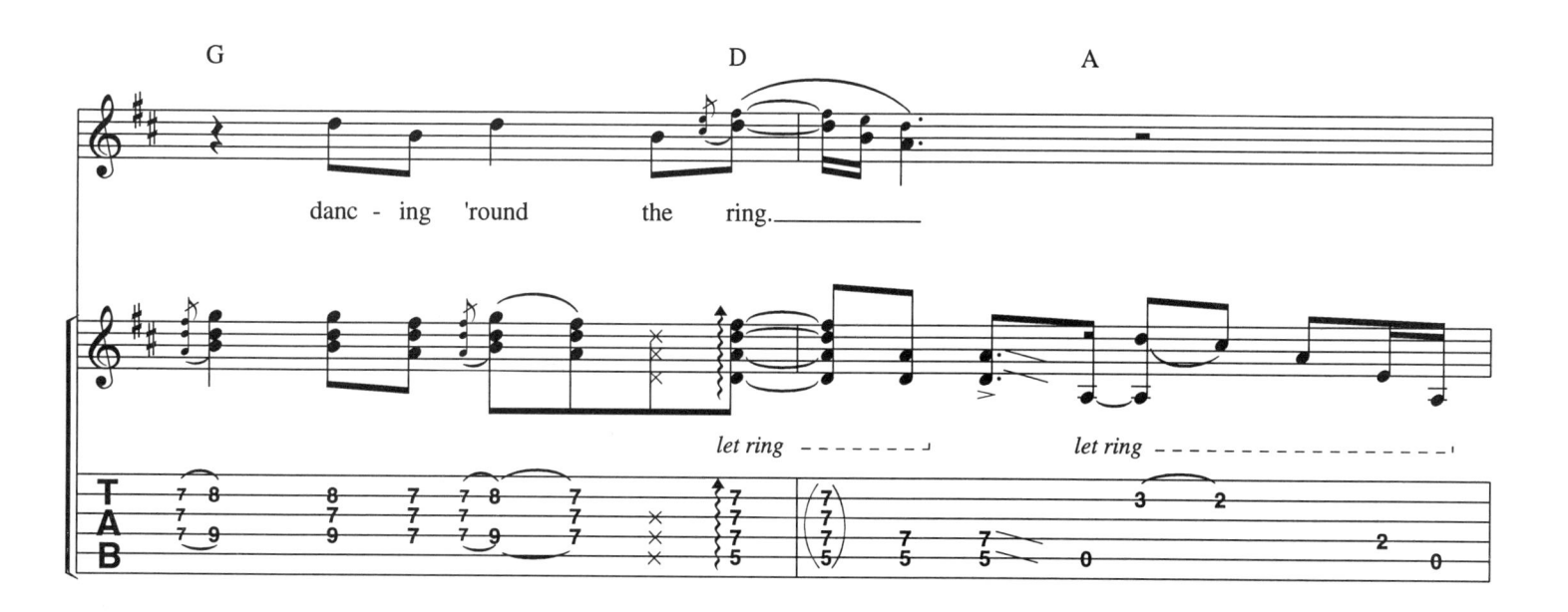

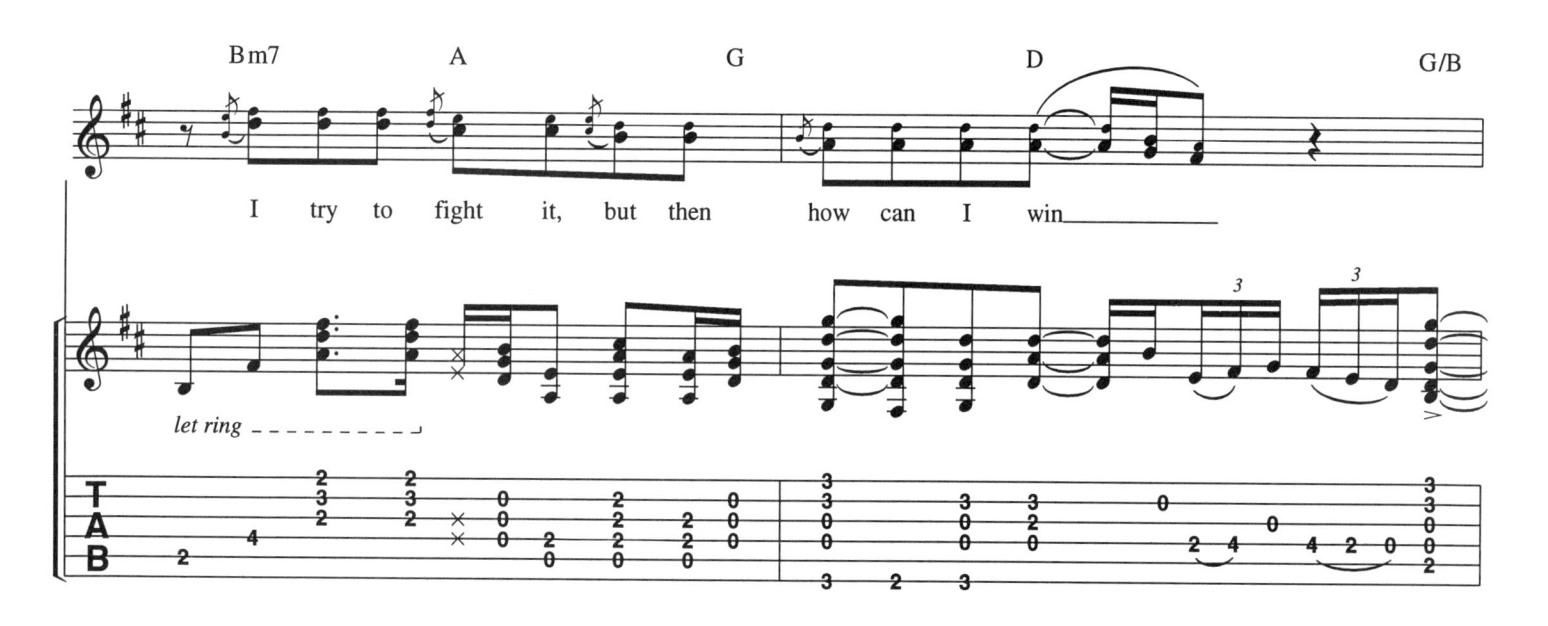

Chorus:

It's just me and my shad - ow____ danc - ing 'round the ring.____ I try to fight it, but then how can I win____

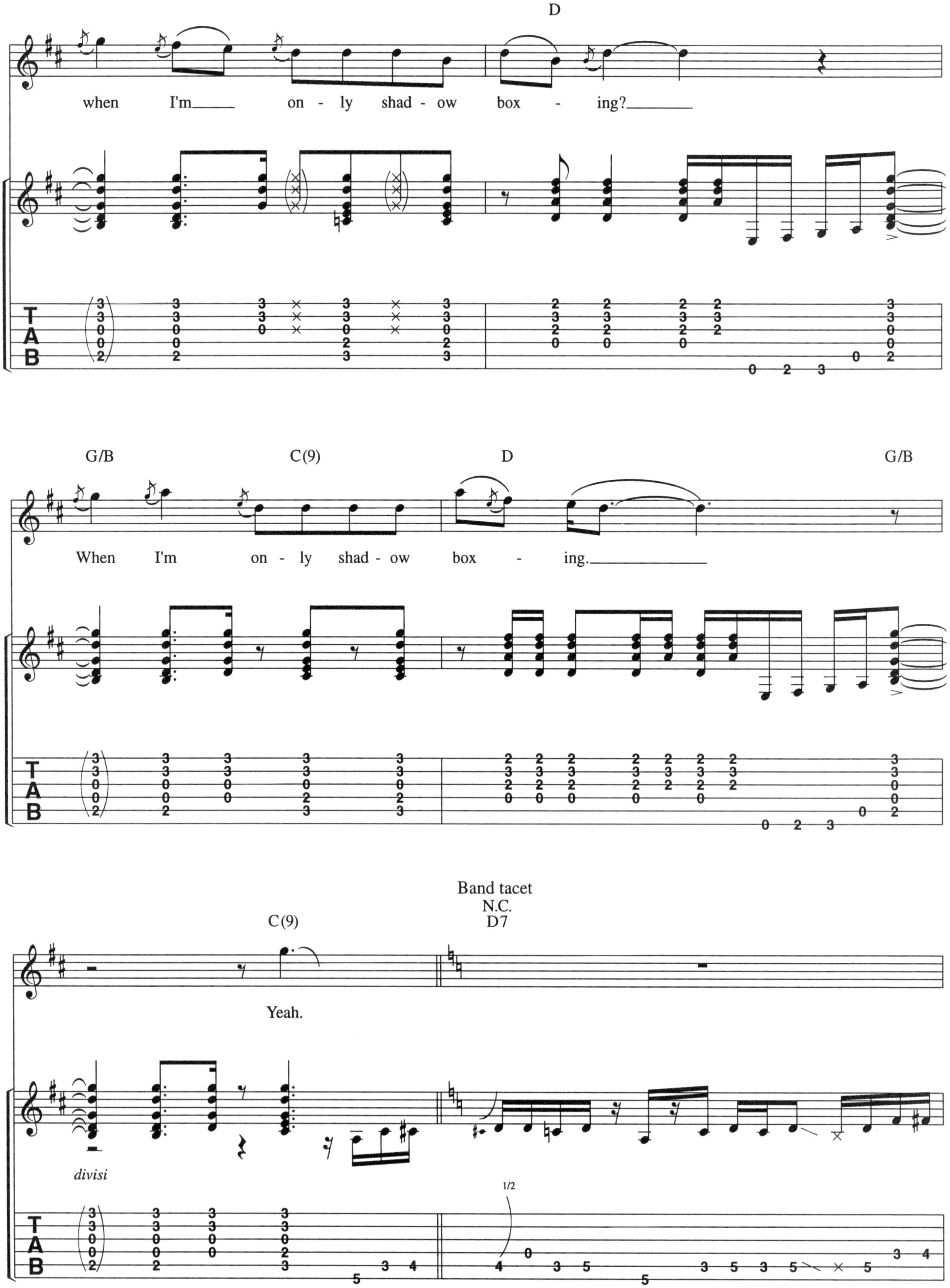
D
when I'm on - ly shad - ow box - ing?
G/B
C(9)
D
G/B
When I'm on - ly shad - ow box - ing.
C(9)
Band tacet
N.C.
D7
Yeah.
divisi
1/2

Shadow Boxing - 13 - 10
PG9515

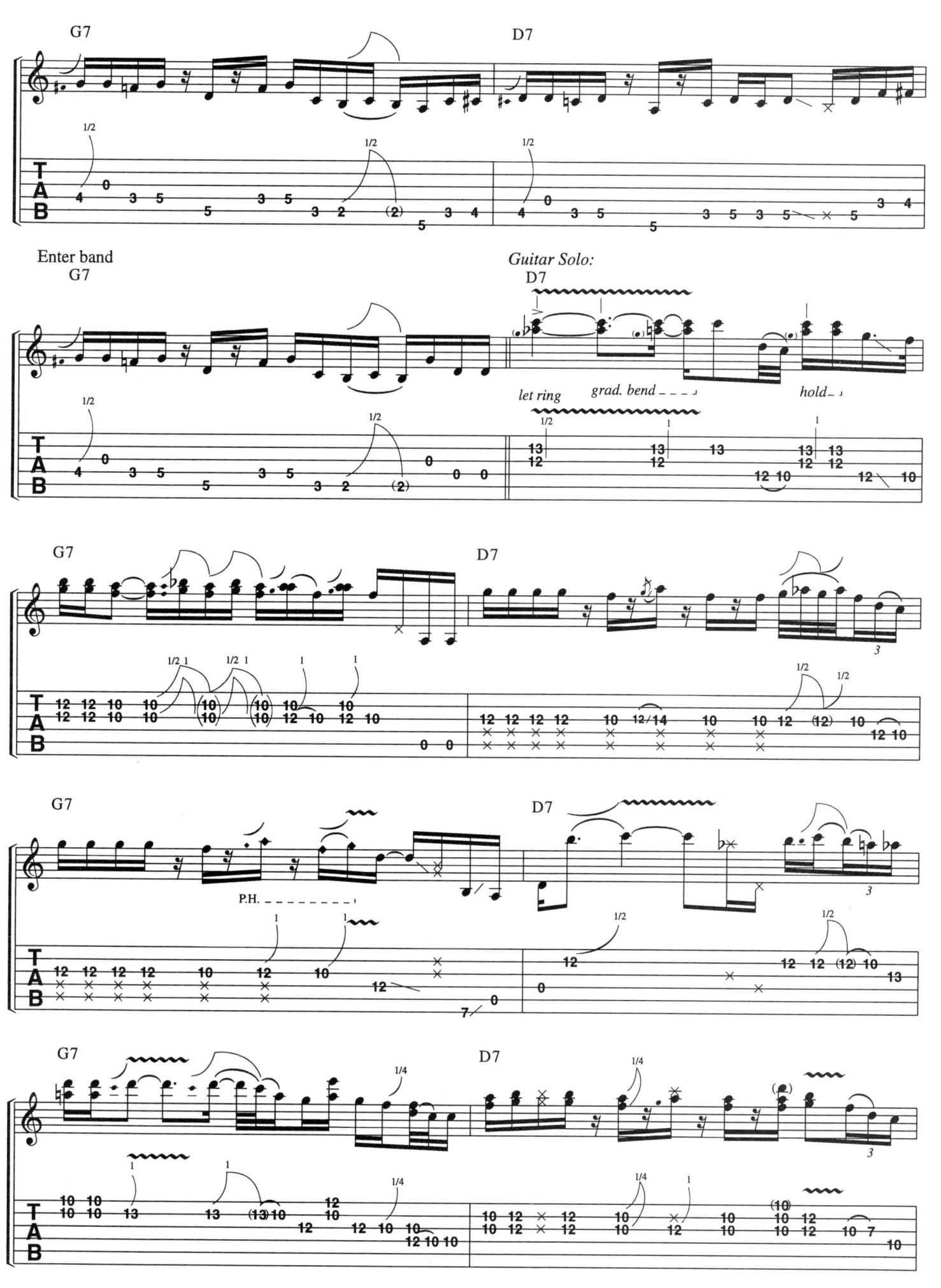

Shadow Boxing - 13 - 11

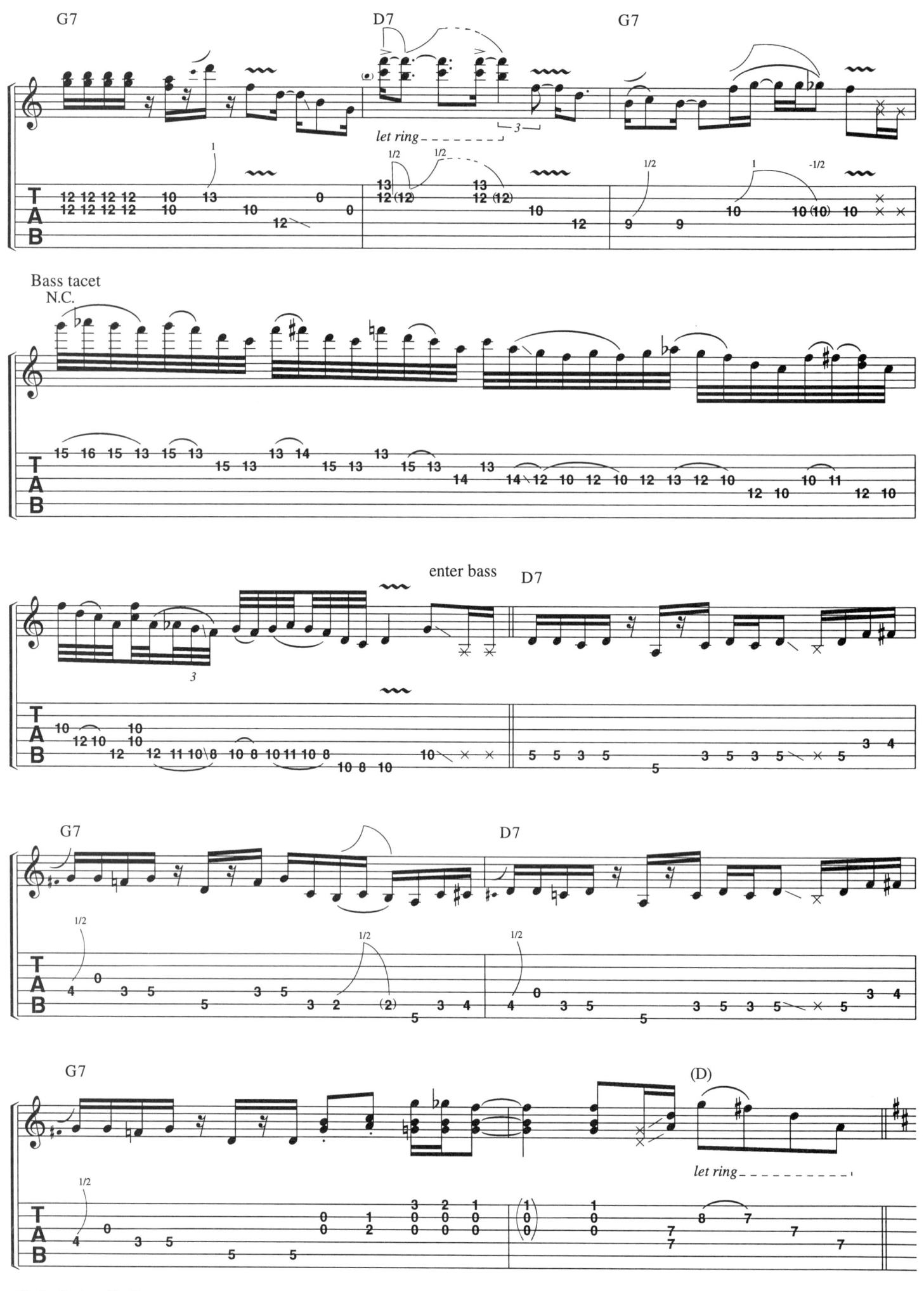

Outro Chorus:
G
D
It's just me and my shad - ow
let ring
G
D
A
danc - ing (a)- round the ring.
let ring
Bm7
A
G
D
G/B
I try to fight it, but how can I win
let ring
3
3

when I'm on - ly shad - ow box - ing?

When I'm on - ly shad - ow box - ing.

Yeah, I'm on - ly.

tell me something i don't know

Words and Music by
NUNO BETTENCOURT/GARY CHERONE/PATRICK BADGER

Tune down 1/2 step:

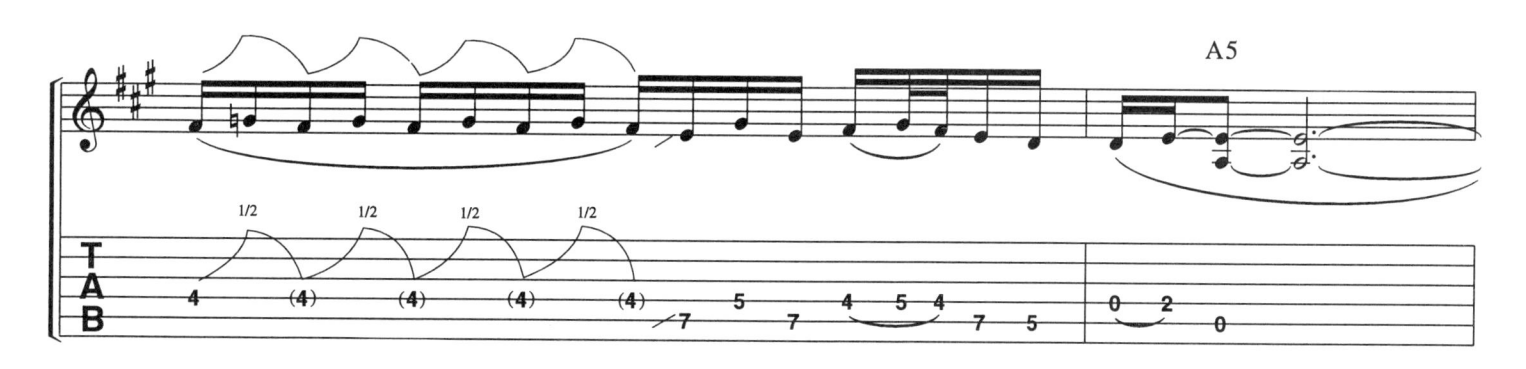

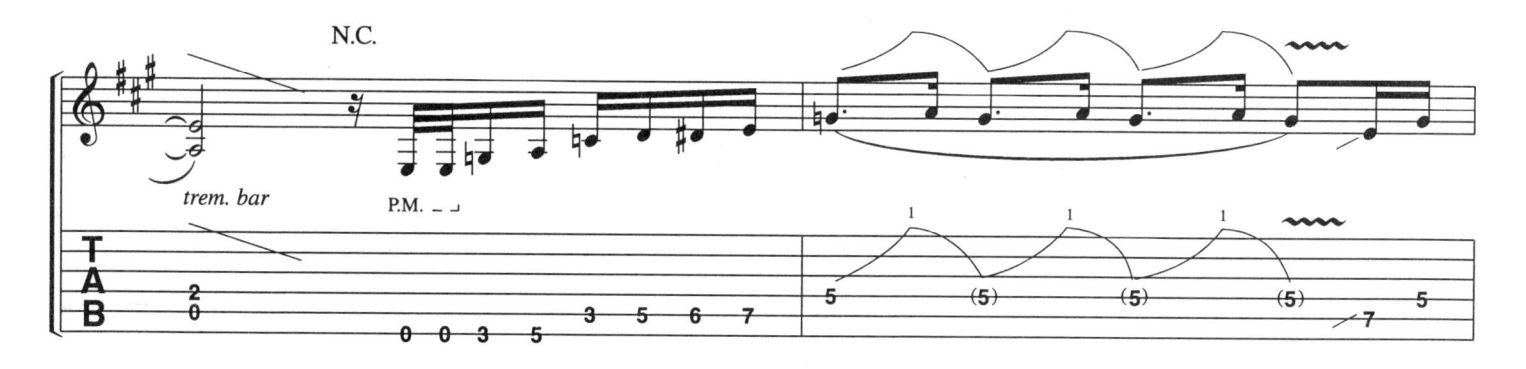

⑥ = E♭   ③ = G♭
⑤ = A♭   ② = B♭
④ = D♭   ① = E♭

Tell Me Something I Don't Know - 11 - 1
PG9515

Copyright © 1995 COLOR ME BLIND MUSIC and PASTY FACE MUSIC (ASCAP)
All Rights Administered by ALMO MUSIC CORP. (ASCAP) Throughout the World Under License from FUNKY METAL MUSIC, INC.
International Copyright Secured   Made in U.S.A.   All Rights Reserved

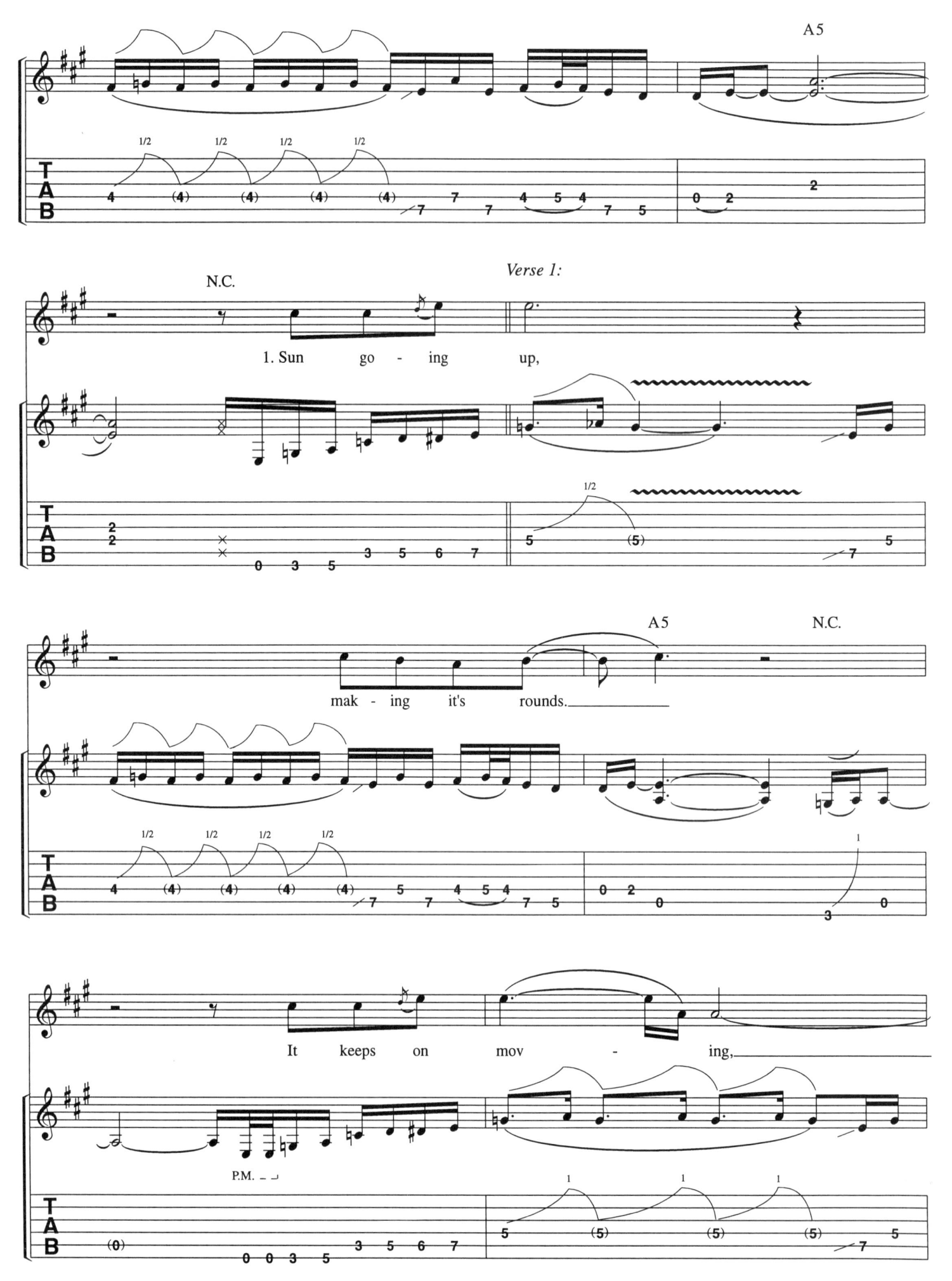

Verse 1:

1. Sun go-ing up, mak-ing it's rounds. It keeps on mov-ing,

Tell Me Something I Don't Know - 11 - 2

105

Tell Me Something I Don't Know - 11 - 3
PG9515

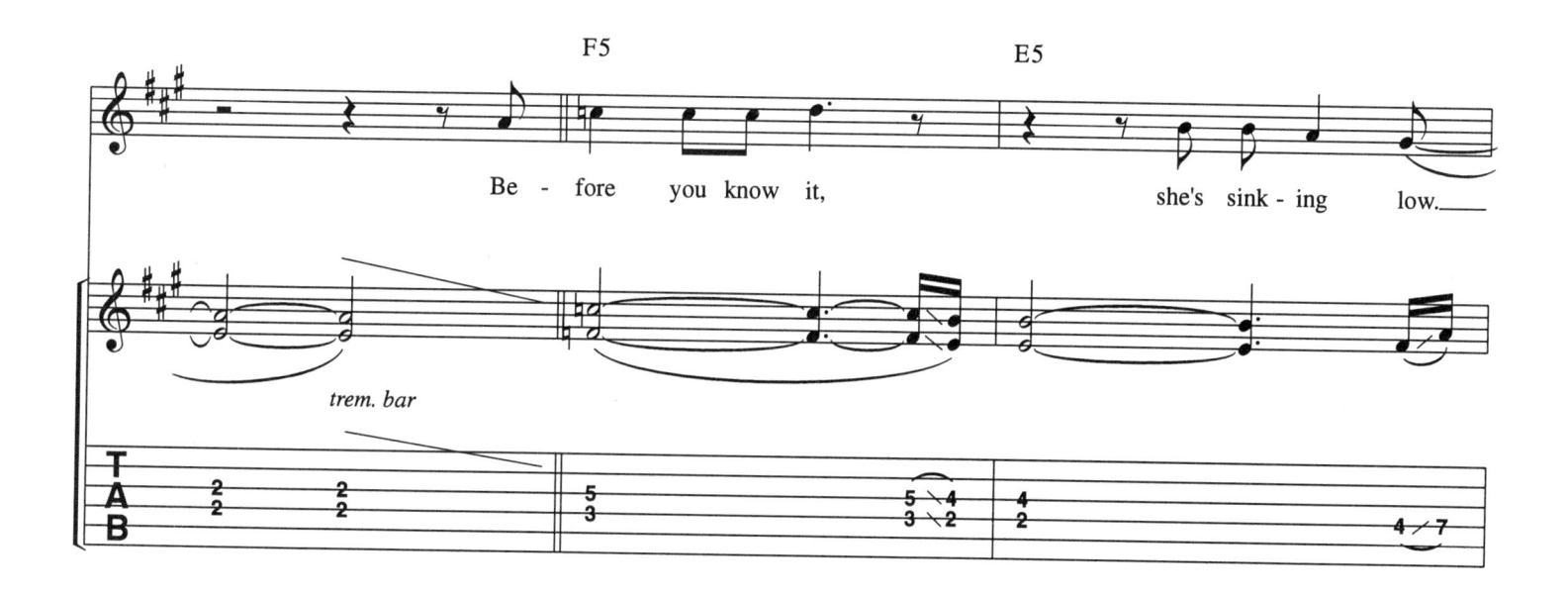

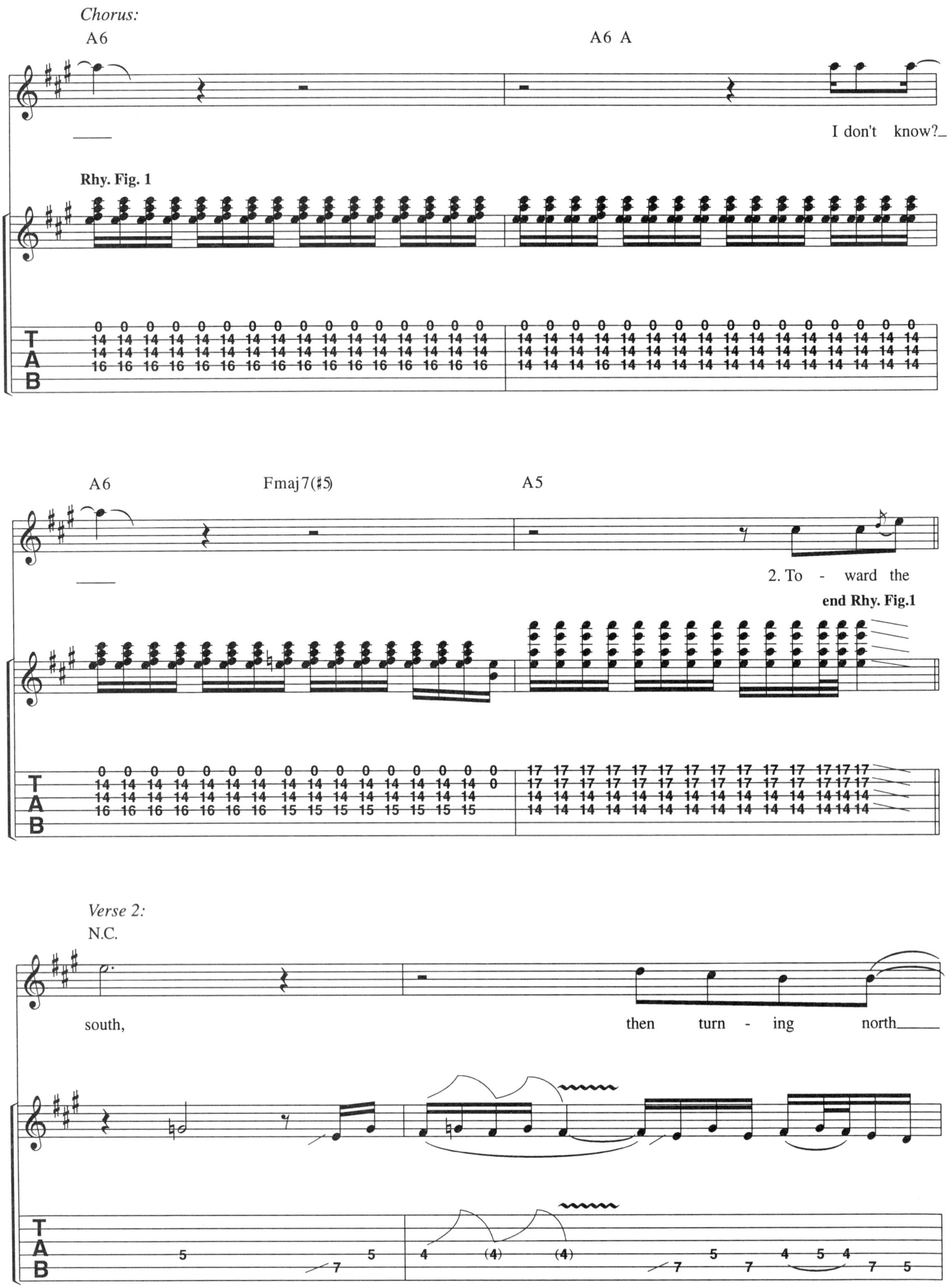
Chorus:
A6
A6 A
I don't know?
Rhy. Fig. 1
A6
Fmaj7(♯5)
A5
2. To - ward the
end Rhy. Fig.1
Verse 2:
N.C.
south,
then turn - ing north

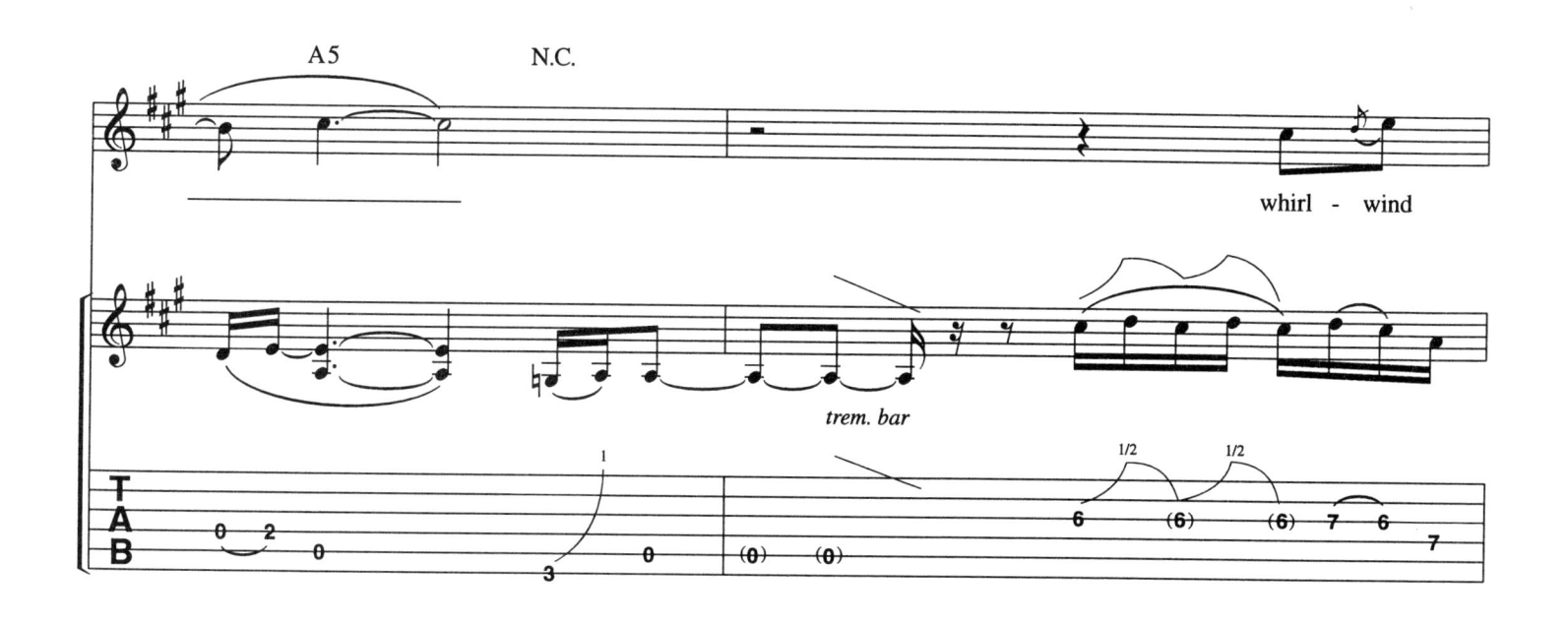

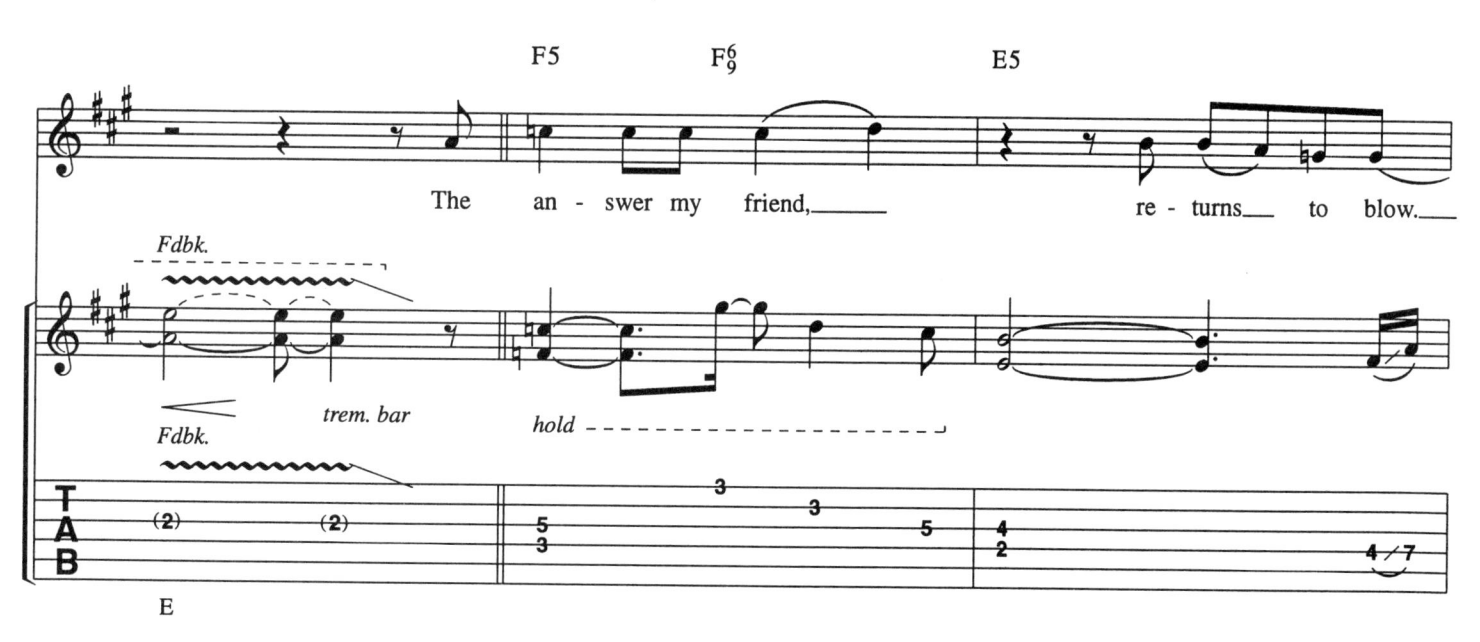

whirl-wind spin-ning on a cir-cu-lar course. The an-swer my friend, re-turns to blow.

Tell Me Something I Don't Know - 11 - 5

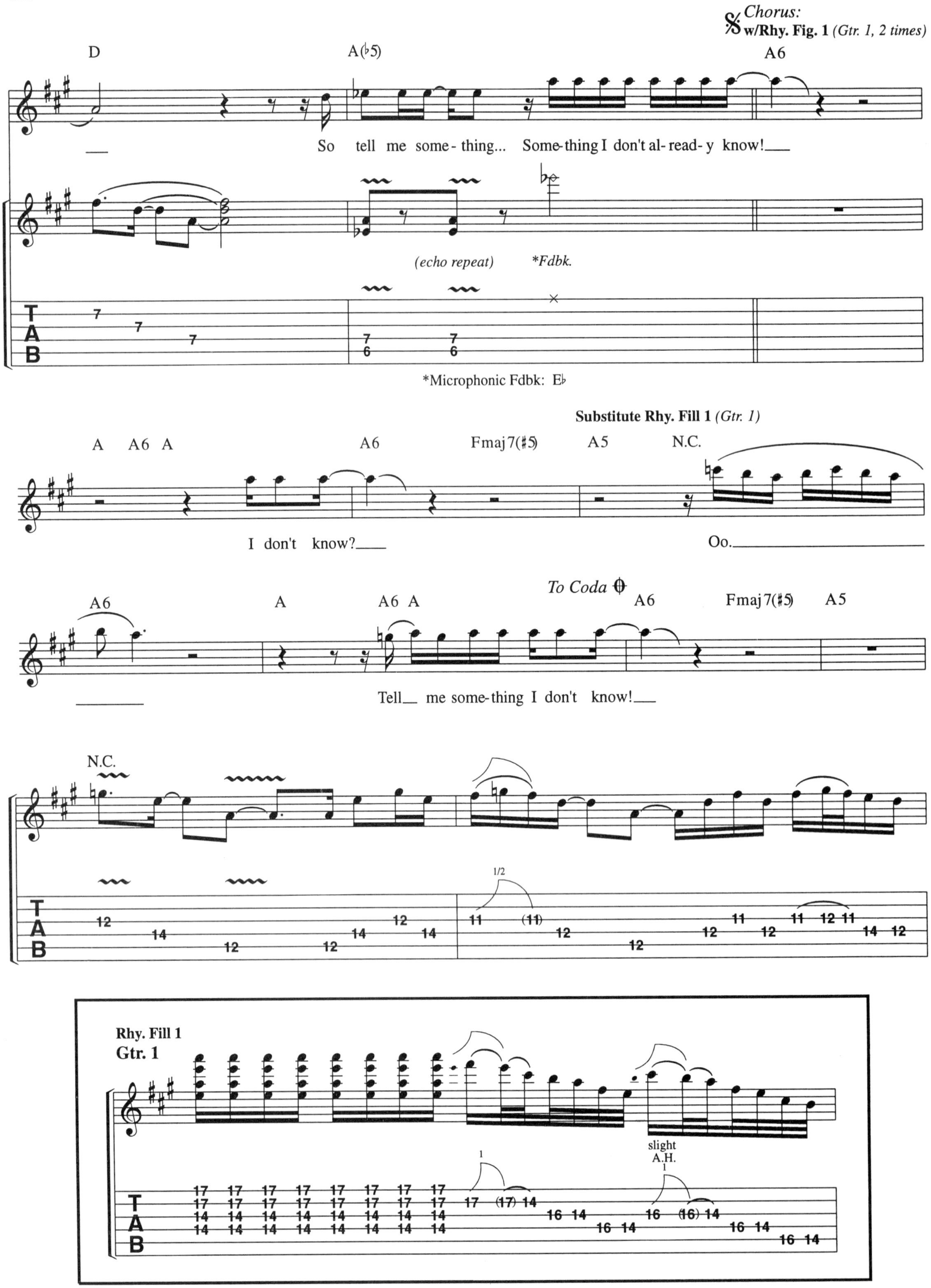
Chorus:
w/Rhy. Fig. 1 (Gtr. 1, 2 times)
D
A(♭5)
A6
So tell me some-thing... Some-thing I don't al-read-y know!
(echo repeat)
*Fdbk.
*Microphonic Fdbk: E♭
Substitute Rhy. Fill 1 (Gtr. 1)
A A6 A
A6
Fmaj7(♯5)
A5
N.C.
I don't know?
Oo.
To Coda
A6
A
A6 A
A6
Fmaj7(♯5)
A5
Tell me some-thing I don't know!
N.C.
Rhy. Fill 1
Gtr. 1
slight
A.H.

Verse 3:

3. As for the wise-men,

(who) pur - sue their know - ledge.

Same as the fool, same as the fool, free fall - ing

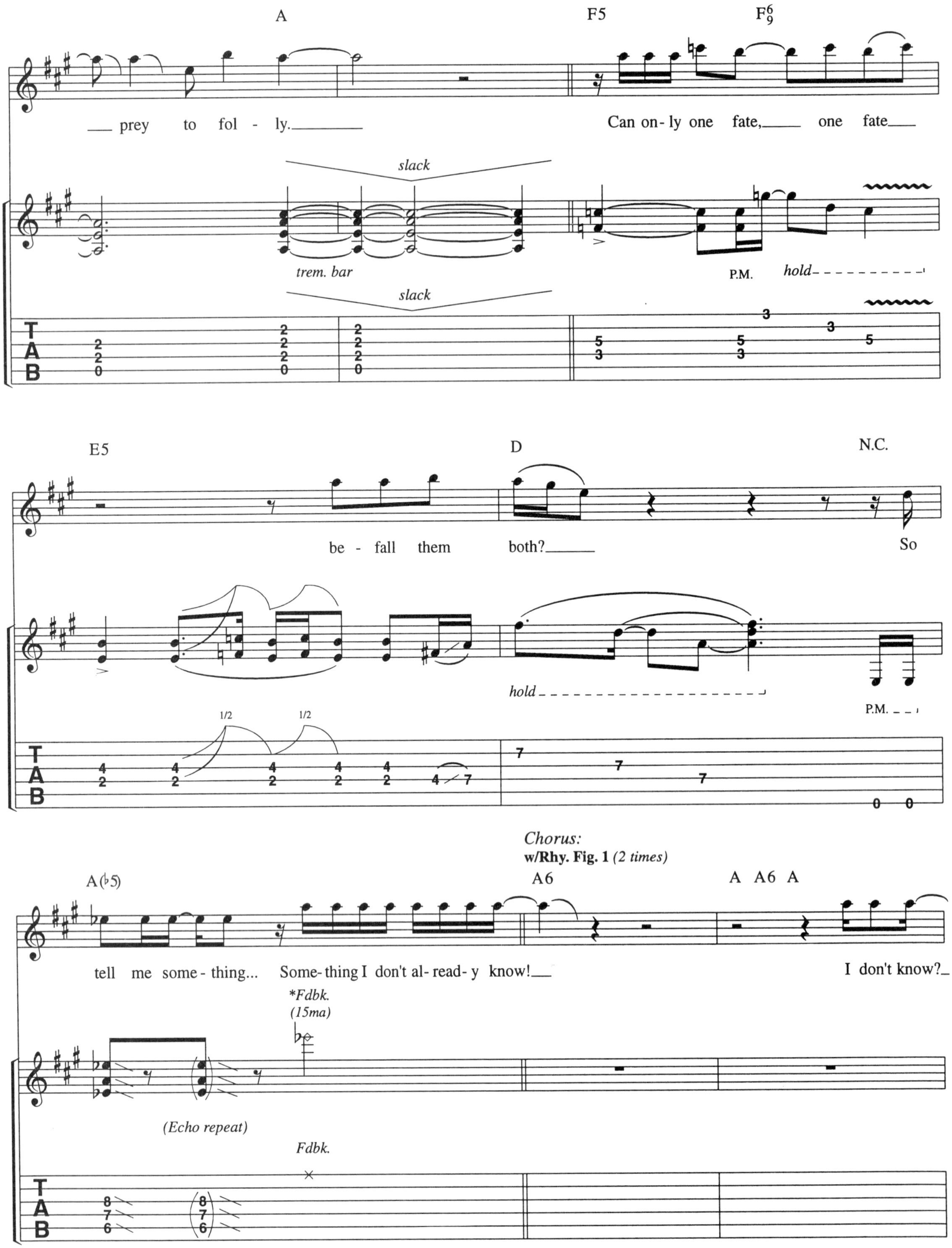

*Microphonic Fdbk: E♭

A6
Fmaj7(♯5)
A5
A6
Oo.
A
A6 A
A6
Fmaj7(♯5)
Tell me something I don't know!
Tell me something I don't know!
A5
Guitar Solo:
N.C.
Ah, can you tell me?
(w/heavy delay = ♩.)
P.M.
P.M.
1/2
trem. bar

1/2
trem. bar
And I must go on,
as for the show.
mp
D.S. 𝄋 al Coda
So tell me some- thing...
Some- thing I don't al - read - y know!

Coda
A6
Fmaj 7(♯5)
A5
Tell___ me some- thing I don't know!____
w/Rhy. Fig. 1 (Gtr. 1, simile)
A6
A
Tell me, tell me, tell me, tell me...
Tell me, tell me, tell___ me, tell me...
A
Fmaj 7(♯5)
A5
Tell me, tell me, tell___ me, tell me...____
Tell me, tell me, tell___ me, tell me!_____
Outro:
Play 5 times
D5
A5
G5
D5

there is no god

Words and Music by
NUNO BETTENCOURT/GARY CHERONE/PATRICK BADGER

115

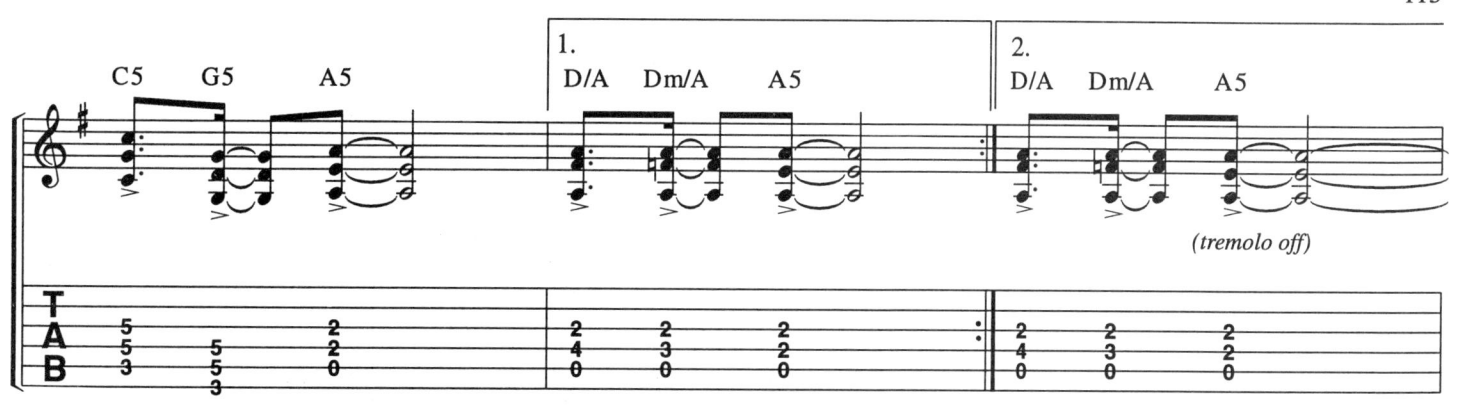

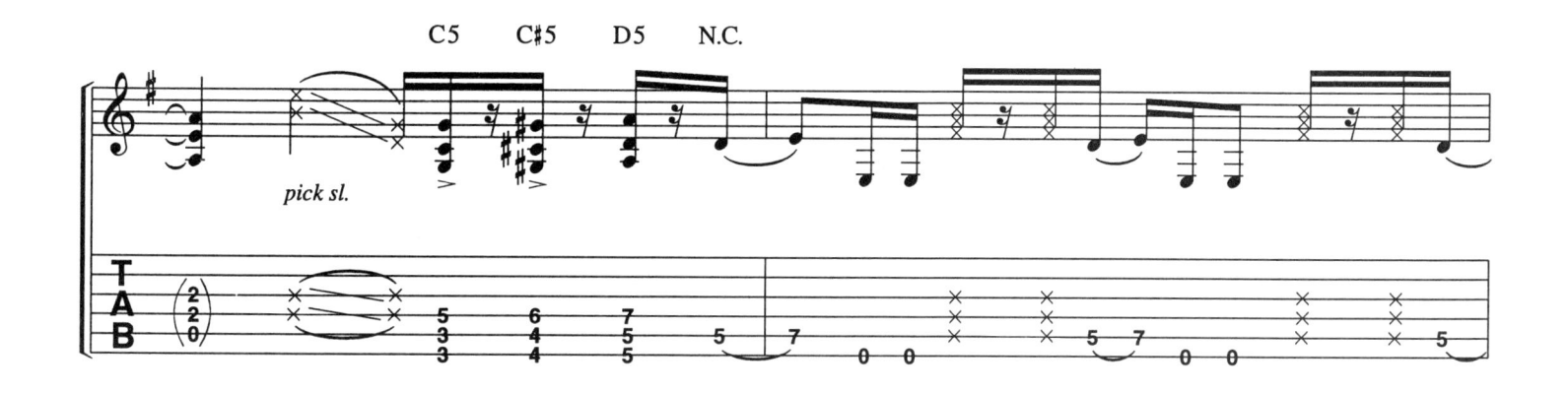

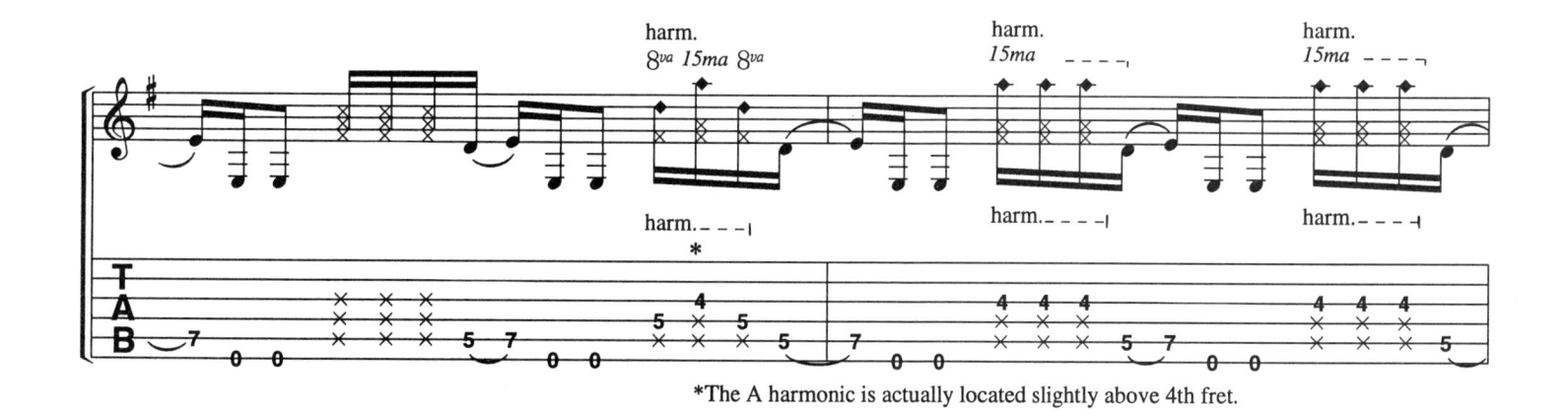

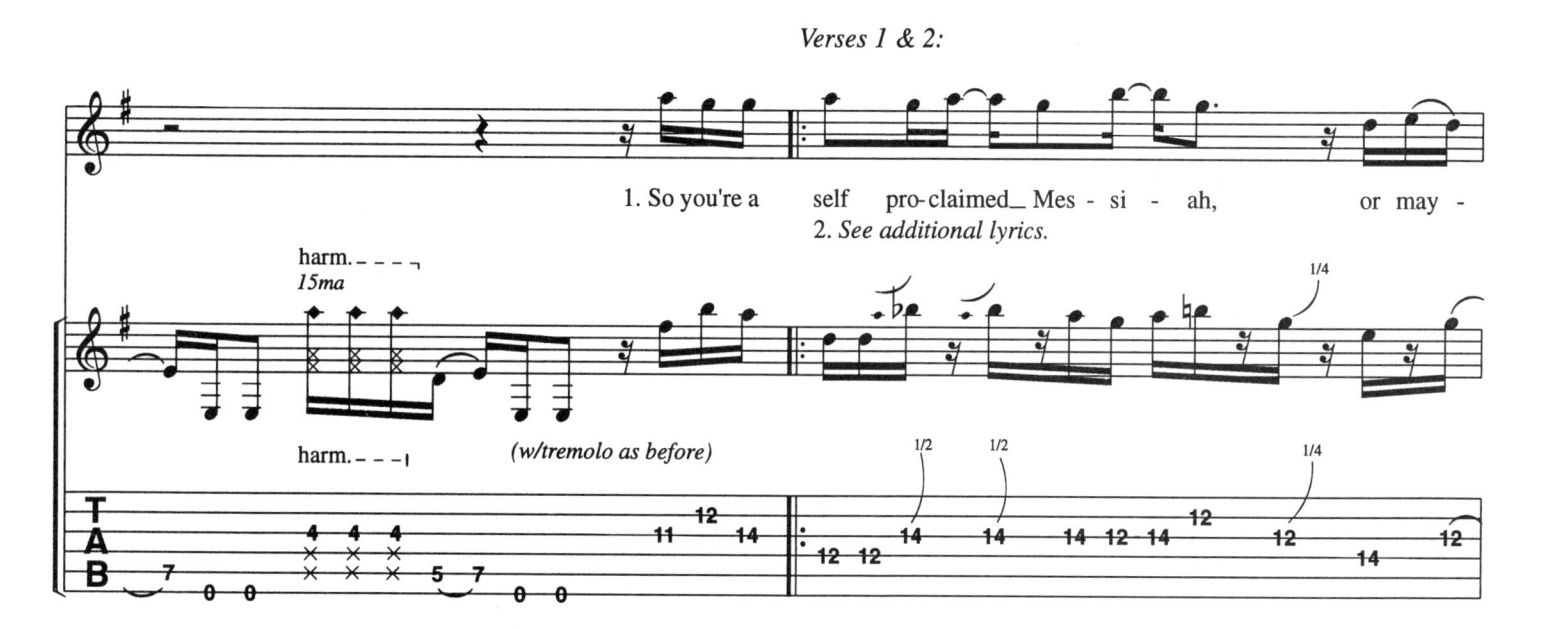

There Is No God - 11 - 3

117

Lyrics:
see that Thom-as wants some proof. Did you come to heal the sick, uh, with one more magician's trick? Ye gen-er-a-tion seeks a sign, ah, while blind keeps lead-ing the blind. So you say there is no God,

Pre - Chorus:

C5 — 1st time: (tied from notation)
G5

2nd time:

(*w/flanger)

*Tremolo off.

There Is No God - 11 - 4
PG9515

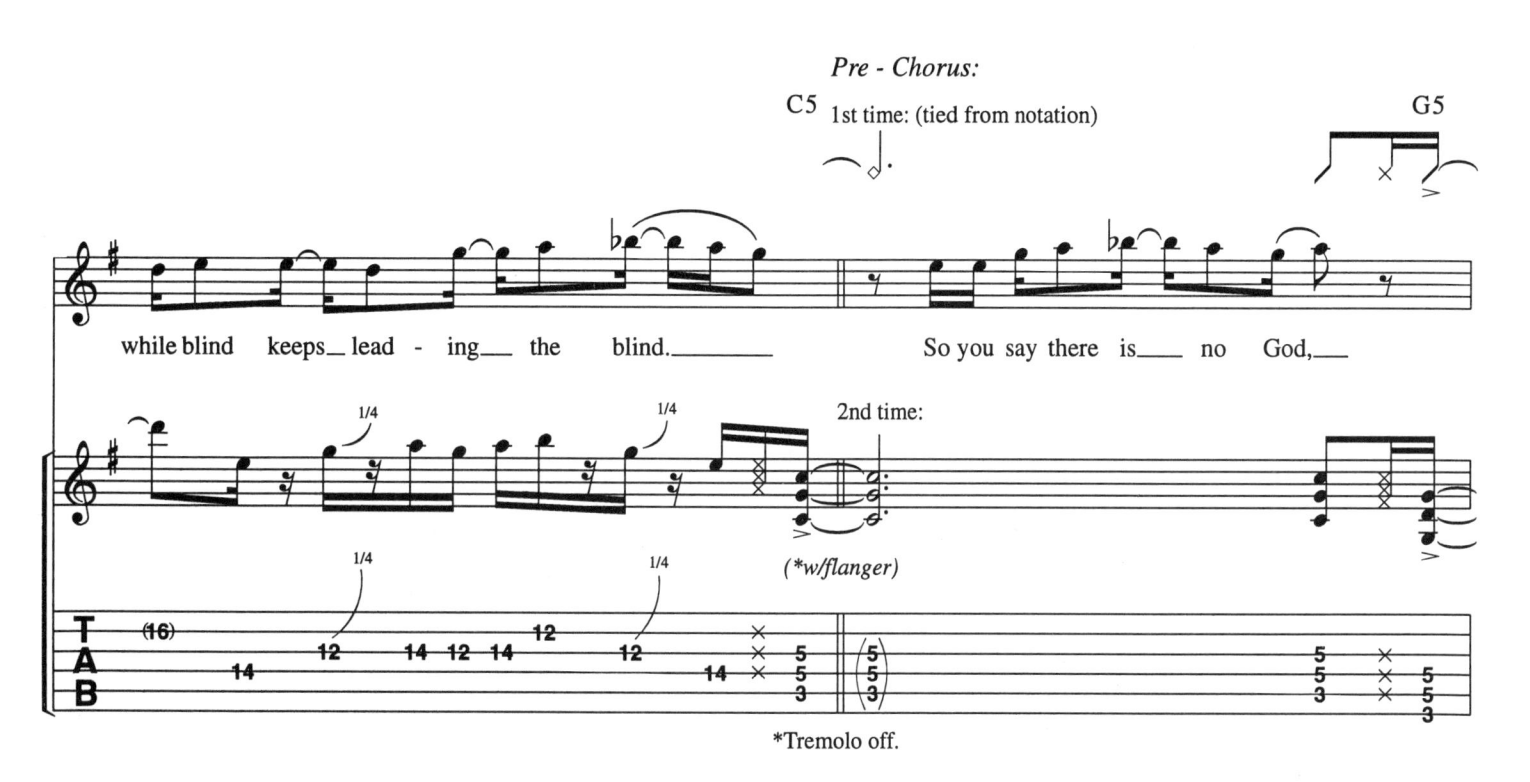

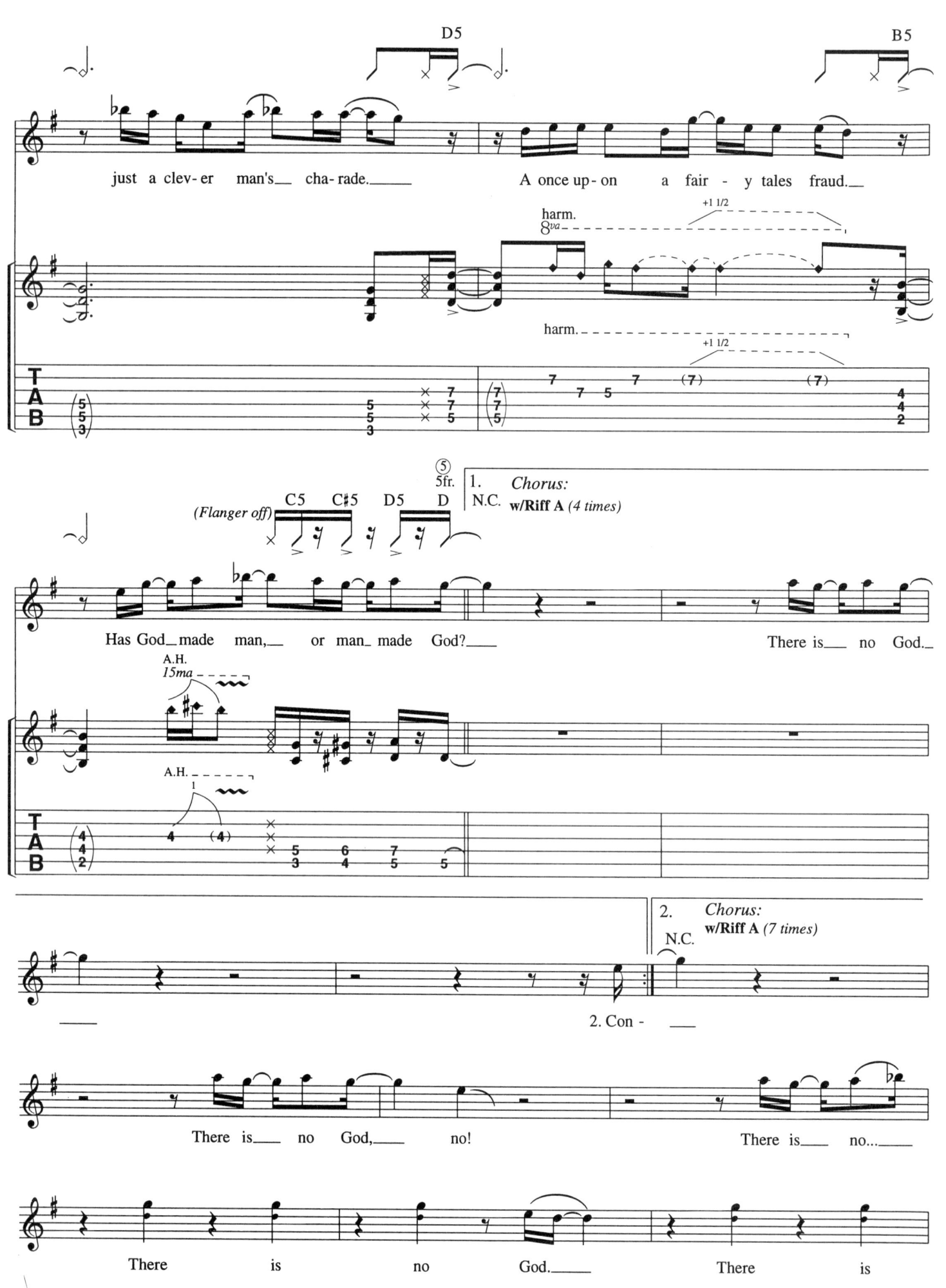

just a clev-er man's cha-rade. A once up-on a fair-y tales fraud.

Chorus:
1. N.C. w/Riff A *(4 times)*

Has God made man, or man made God? There is no God.

Chorus:
2. N.C. w/Riff A *(7 times)*

2. Con-

There is no God, no! There is no...

There is no God. There is

*Point bar backward and bounce w/right hand in indicated rhythm.

A.H. pitch: B / C# \ B

There Is No God - 11 - 6
PG9515

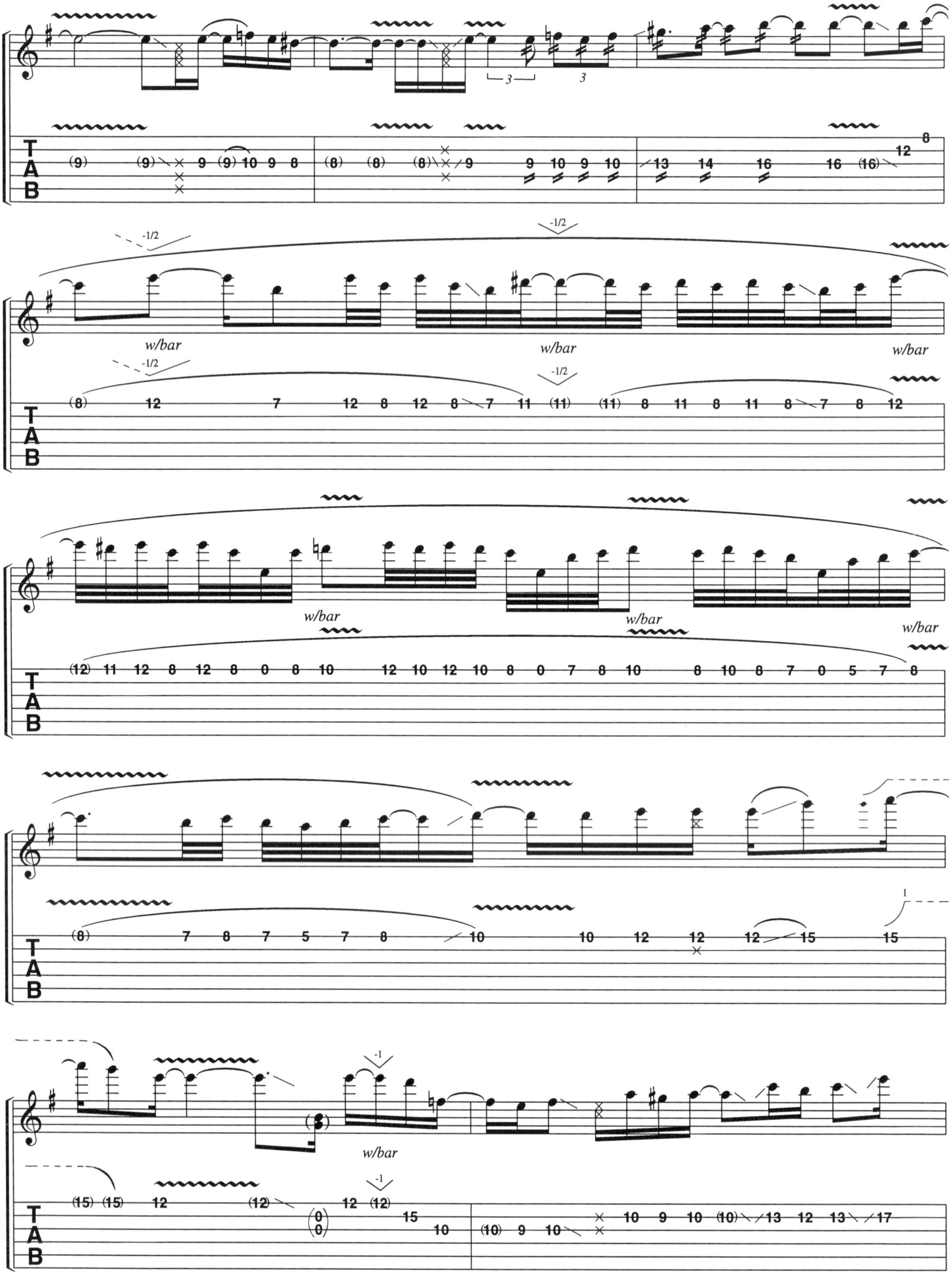
-1/2
w/bar
-1/2
w/bar
w/bar
w/bar
w/bar
w/bar
-1
w/bar
-1

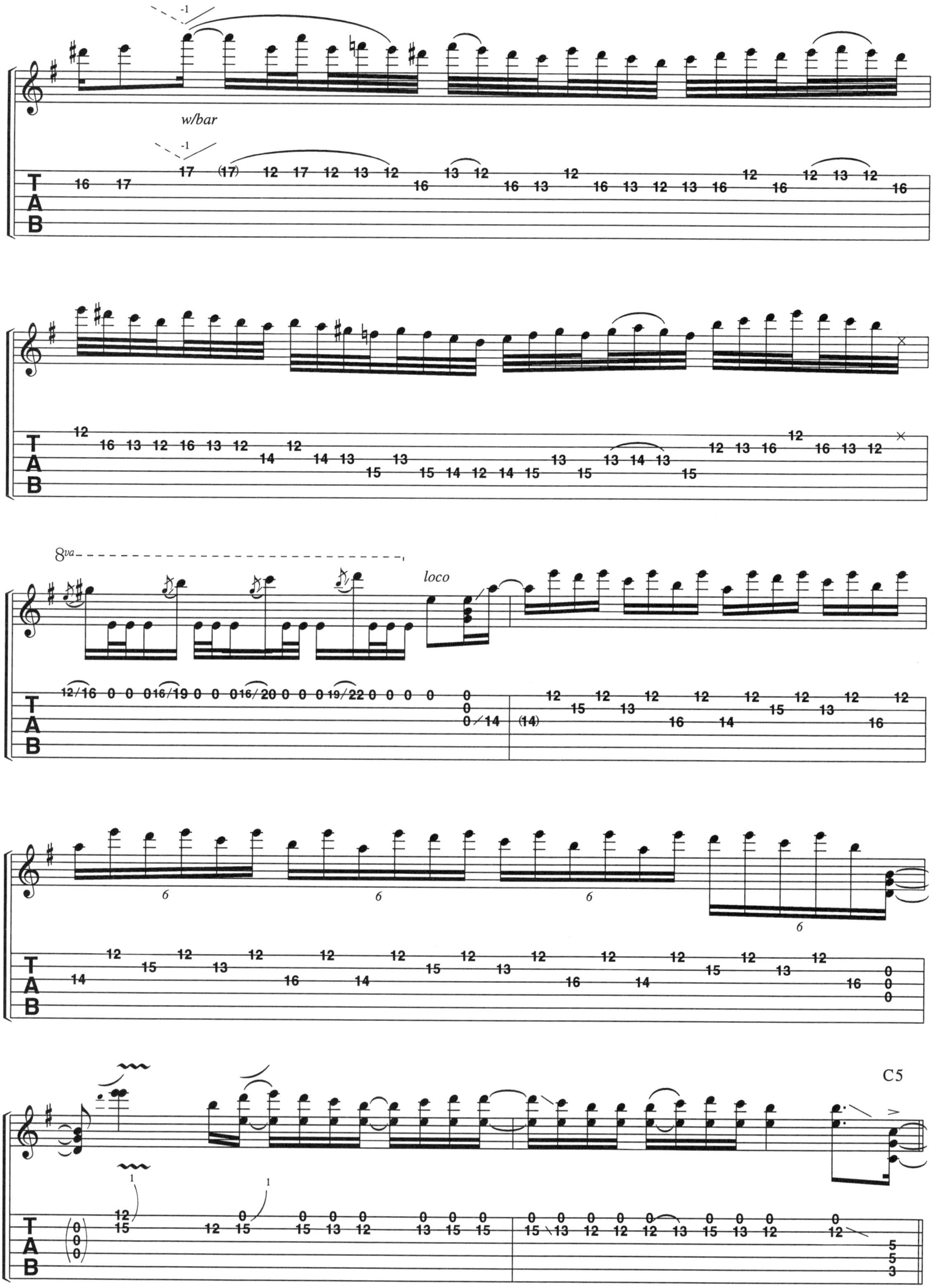
w/bar
8va
loco
C5

Pre - Chorus:
G5
D5
Oo, so you say there is no God.
(It's just a clev- er man's cha - rade,
D
Bm7
C5 C♯5 D5
Ah, once up- on a fair - y tale fraud.
ah.)
Has God made man made God made man
harm.
harm.
G5 F♯5 F5 N.C.
Chorus:
w/Riff A (5 times)
or man made God?
There is no God,
no!
There is no...
There is

Bm7(11) Cm7(11) C♯m7(11) E7sus
no God.
There is
Gtr. 1
Bm7(11) Cm7(11) C♯m7(11) E7sus
no God.
There is
Bm7(11) Cm7(11) C♯m7(11) E7sus
no God.
There is

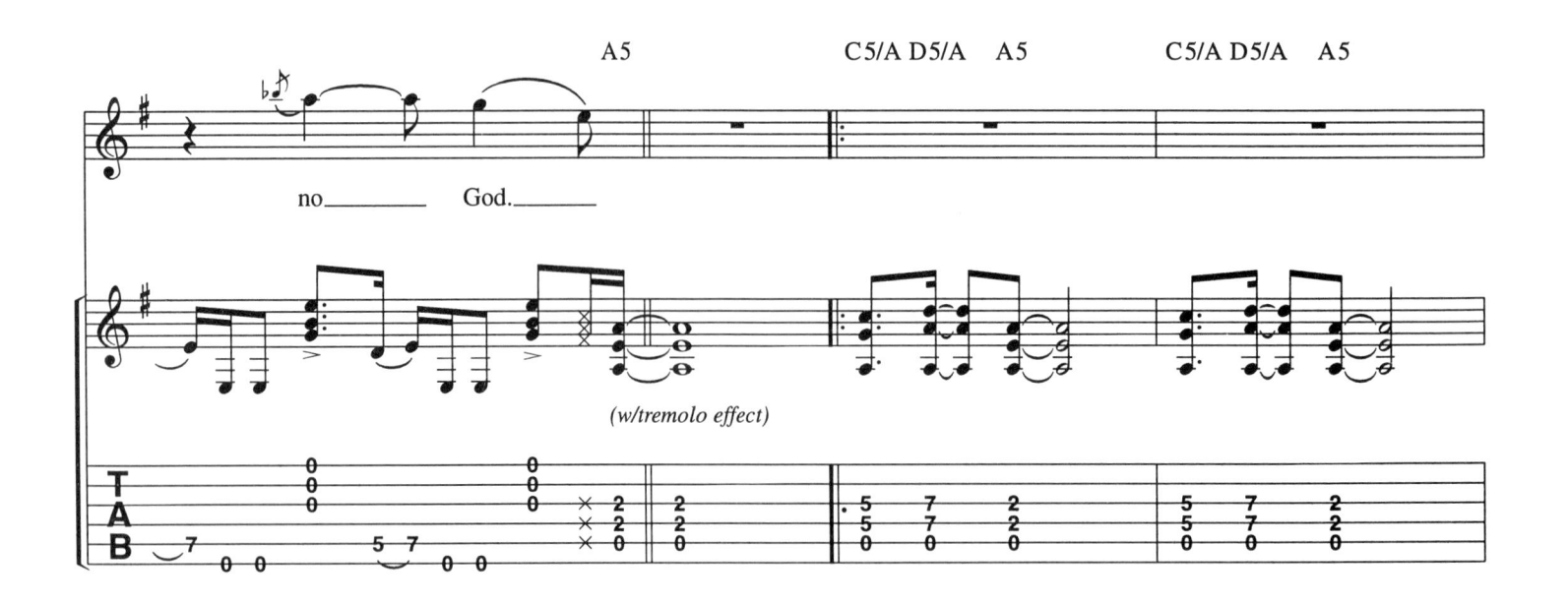

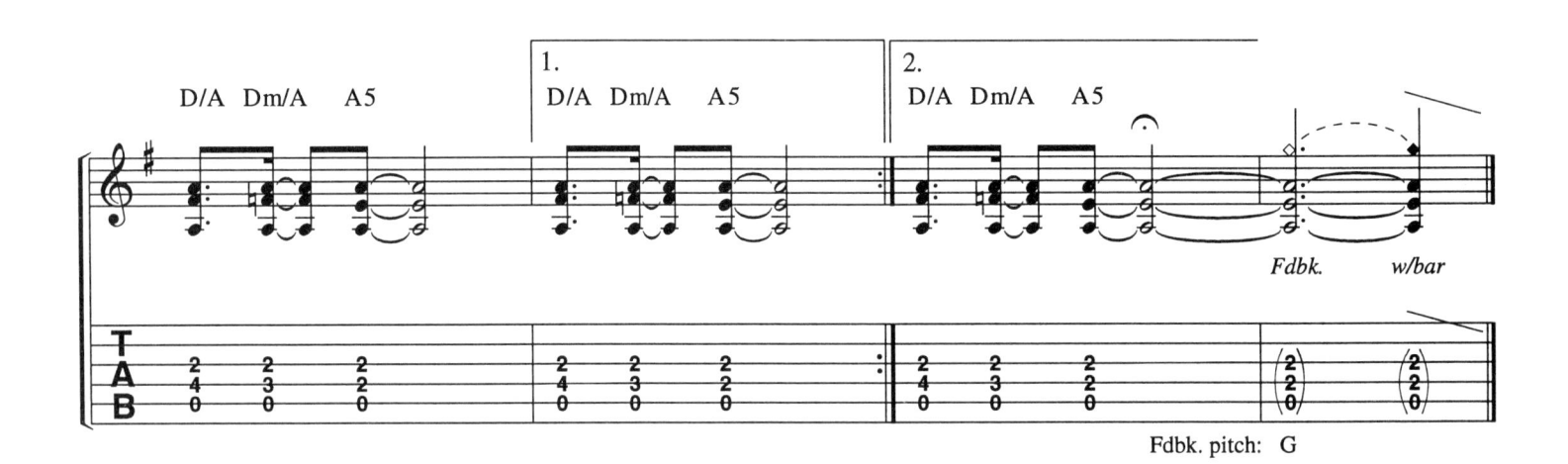

Verse 2:
Confused, thy talk in parables,
Accused, thou walk in parallels.
A simple game of Simon Says,
This month's flavor: sciences.
Today's fact, tomorrow's fiction,
Leave the rest to superstition.
If knowledge comes from learning books,
Wisdom from discerning looks.
A fool that says there is no God,
Don't feel for that sorry sod.
Who needs proof, then he'll believe.
I wonder if he's been deceived.
(To Chorus:)

waiting for the punchline

All gtrs. tune down 1/2 step:
⑥ = E♭ ③ = G♭
⑤ = A♭ ② = B♭
④ = D♭ ① = E♭
Gtr. 1, 6th string = D♭

Words and Music by
NUNO BETTENCOURT/GARY CHERONE

Moderately ♩ = 84
Intro:

Verse:
N.C.
A7

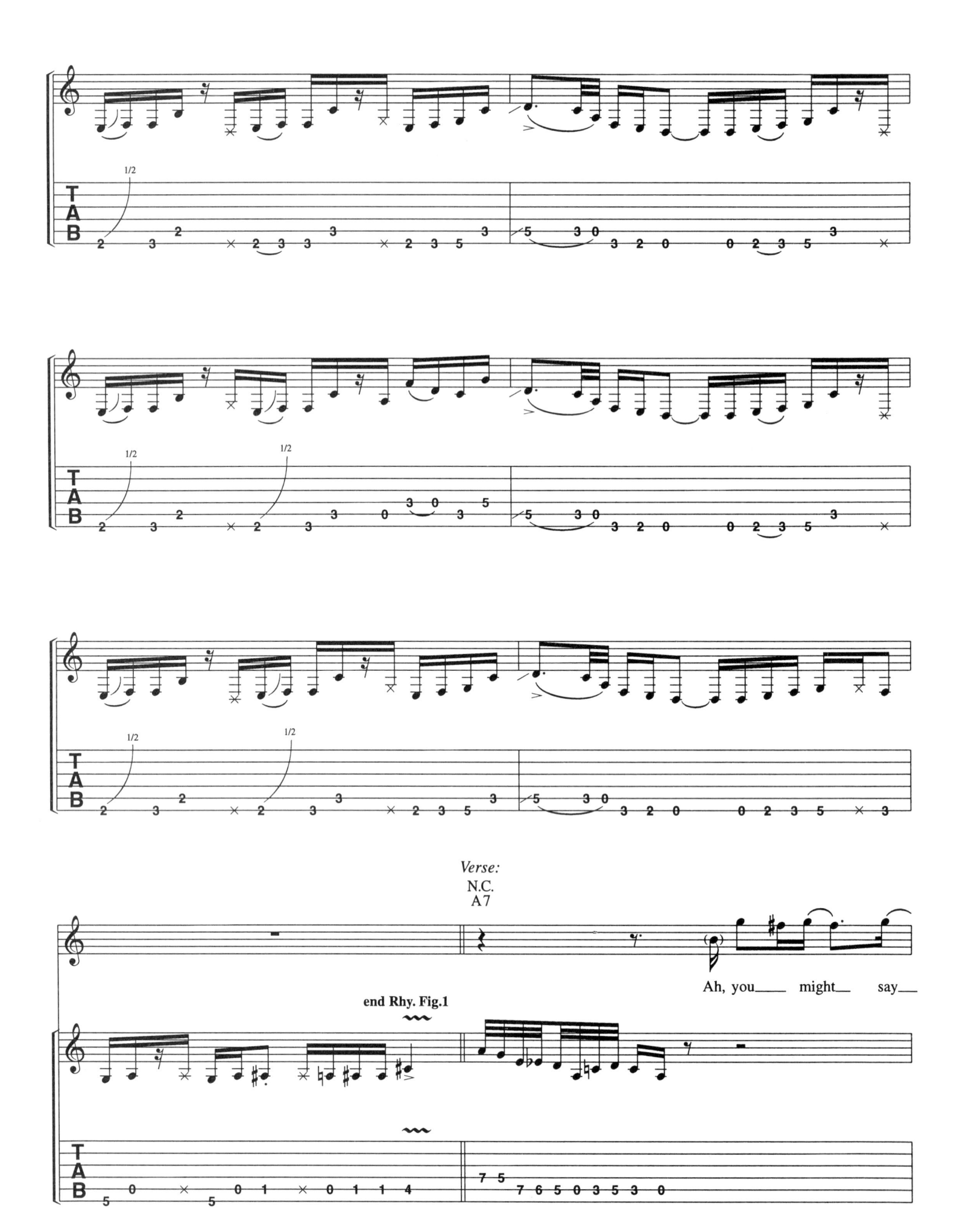

Ah, you___ might___ say___

end Rhy. Fig.1

hey_____ I lost my sense of hu - mor._____ Well, I'm quite__ sur-

prised____ I did-n't lose it soon-er._____ Ah, why__ waste__ my__

__ breath_____ on__ an-y-thing____ less_____ than talk so triv-i-al.____

Waiting For The Punchline - 13 - 3
PG9515

128

As a man who ran out of ma - te - ri - al.

Chorus:
w/Rhy. Fig. 1 *(Gtr. 1, Substitute Fill 1 in bar 6)*

N.C.
(Dm)

Vcl. Fig. 1

Why did the chick-en go a-cross the road.___ To get to the oth - er side.___

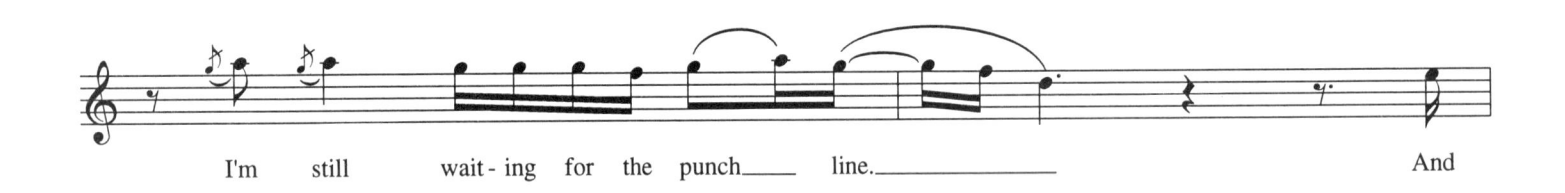

I'm still wait-ing for the punch___ line.___ And

end Vcl. Fig. 1

who - ev - er said the grass al - ways grows___ green - er on the oth - er, lied.___

Fill 1

Waiting For The Punchline - 13 - 4
PG9515

129

Verse:
N.C.
(A7)

I'm still waiting for the punch line. 2. The good old days I was known to wear a smile. Well, like all good things, they've gone out of style. I will ad-

G5 A5   G5 A5   D/F#   N.C.
(A7)

Waiting For The Punchline - 13 - 5
PG9515

mit____ I'm us-ual-ly a quick____ wit____ I find be__ mus - ing.__

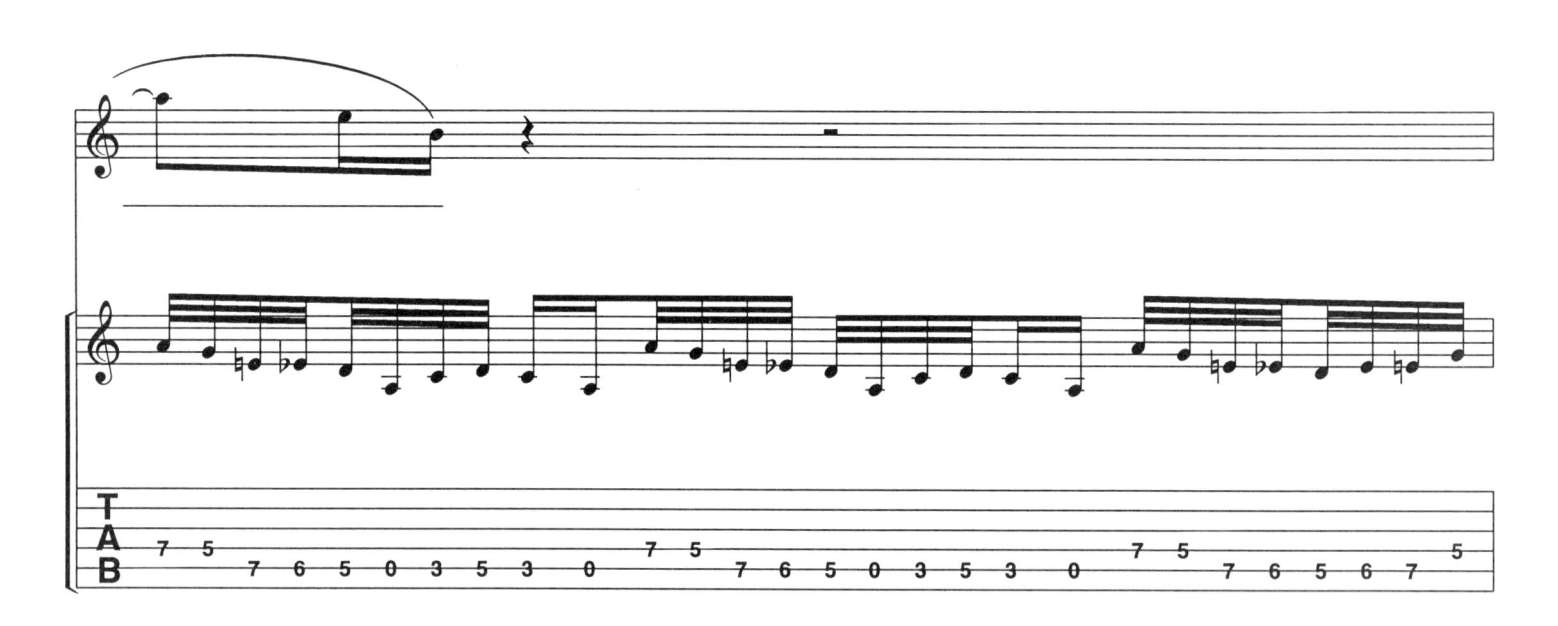

What used to be,___ no long - er are__ a - mus - ing.__

Chorus:
w/Rhy. Fig. 1 *(Gtr. 1, substitute Fill 2 in bar 6)*

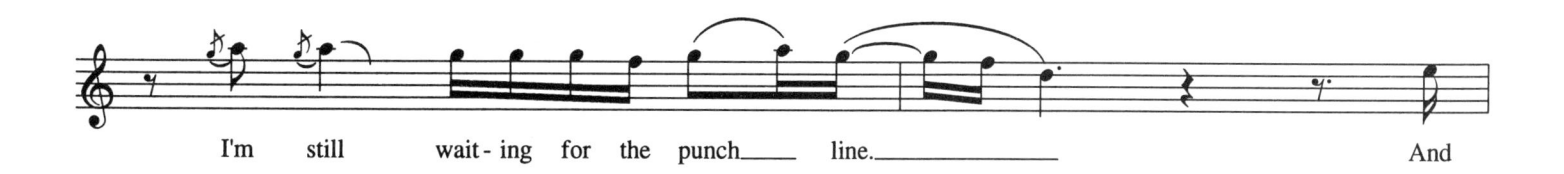

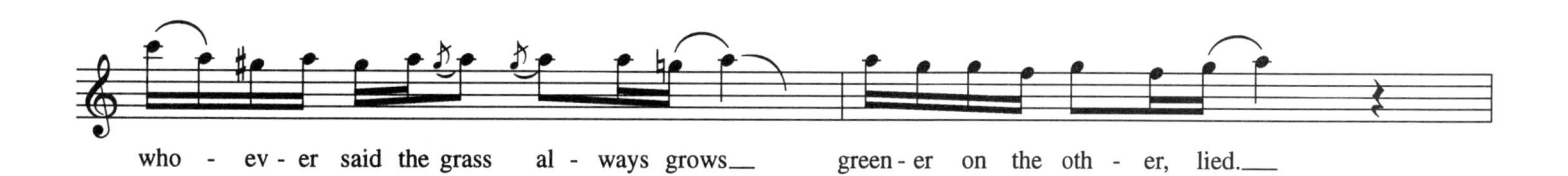

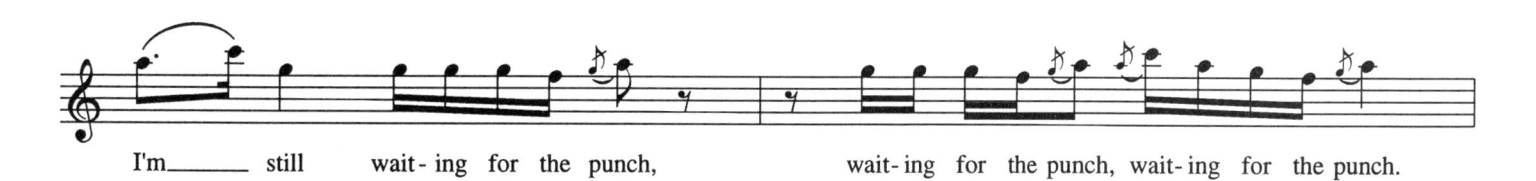

Why did the chick-en go a-cross the road.__ To get to the oth-er side.__

I'm still wait-ing for the punch__ line._____ And

who-ev-er said the grass al-ways grows__ green-er on the oth-er, lied.__

I'm____ still wait-ing for the punch, wait-ing for the punch, wait-ing for the punch.

Instrumental Interlude:
Band tacet
N.C.
(Dm)

Gtr. 1

Rhy. Fill 2
Gtr. 1

mf

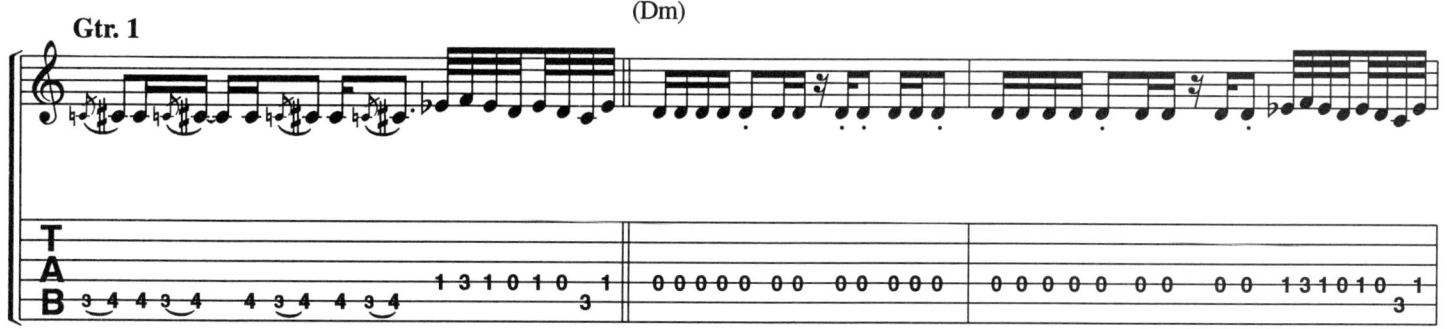

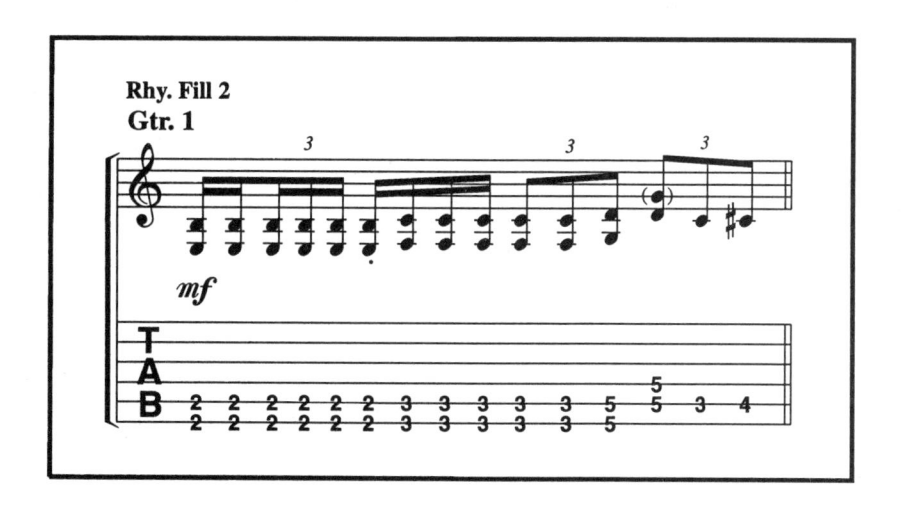

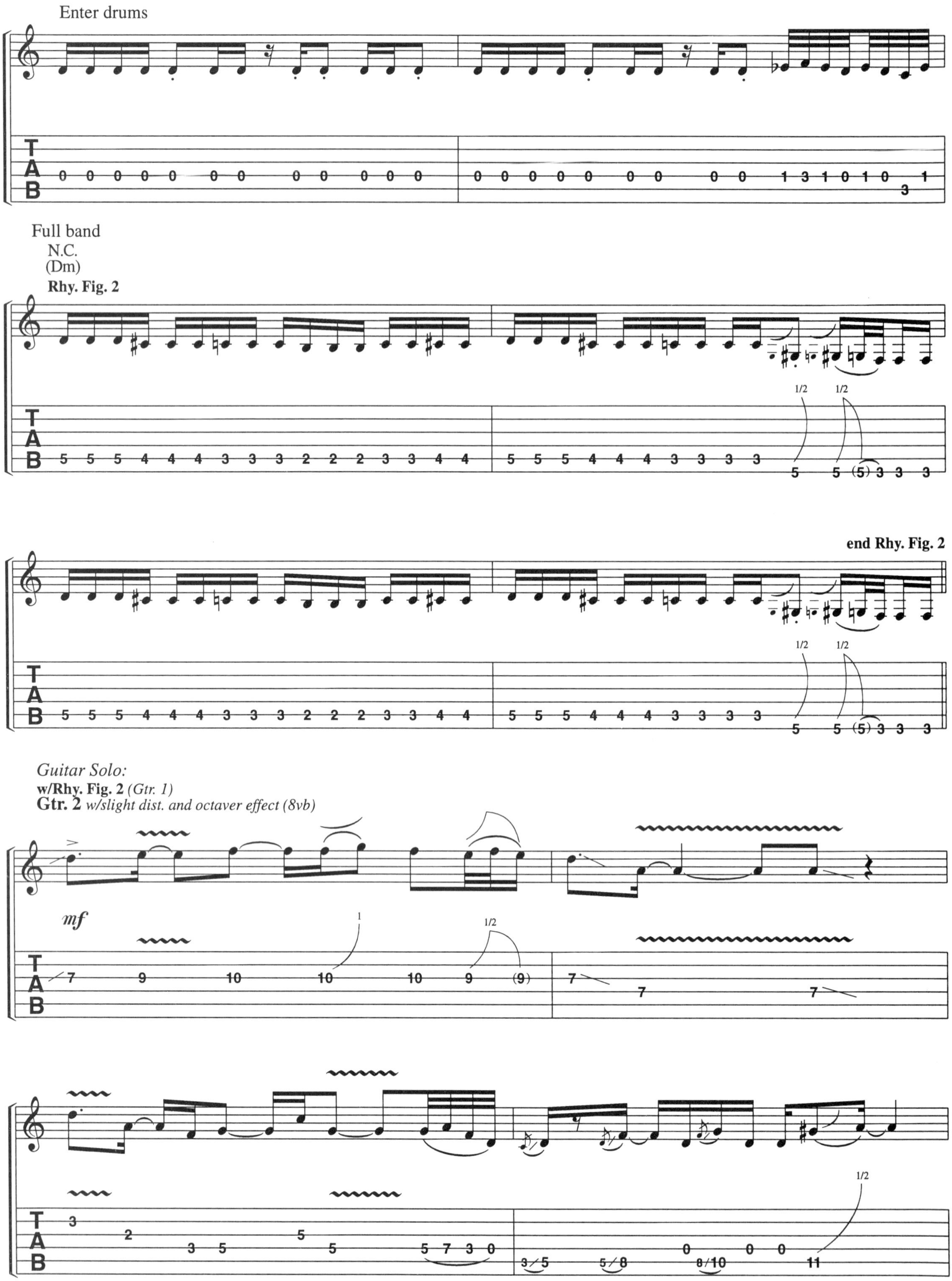
Enter drums
Full band
N.C.
(Dm)
Rhy. Fig. 2
end Rhy. Fig. 2
Guitar Solo:
w/Rhy. Fig. 2 (Gtr. 1)
Gtr. 2 w/slight dist. and octaver effect (8vb)
mf

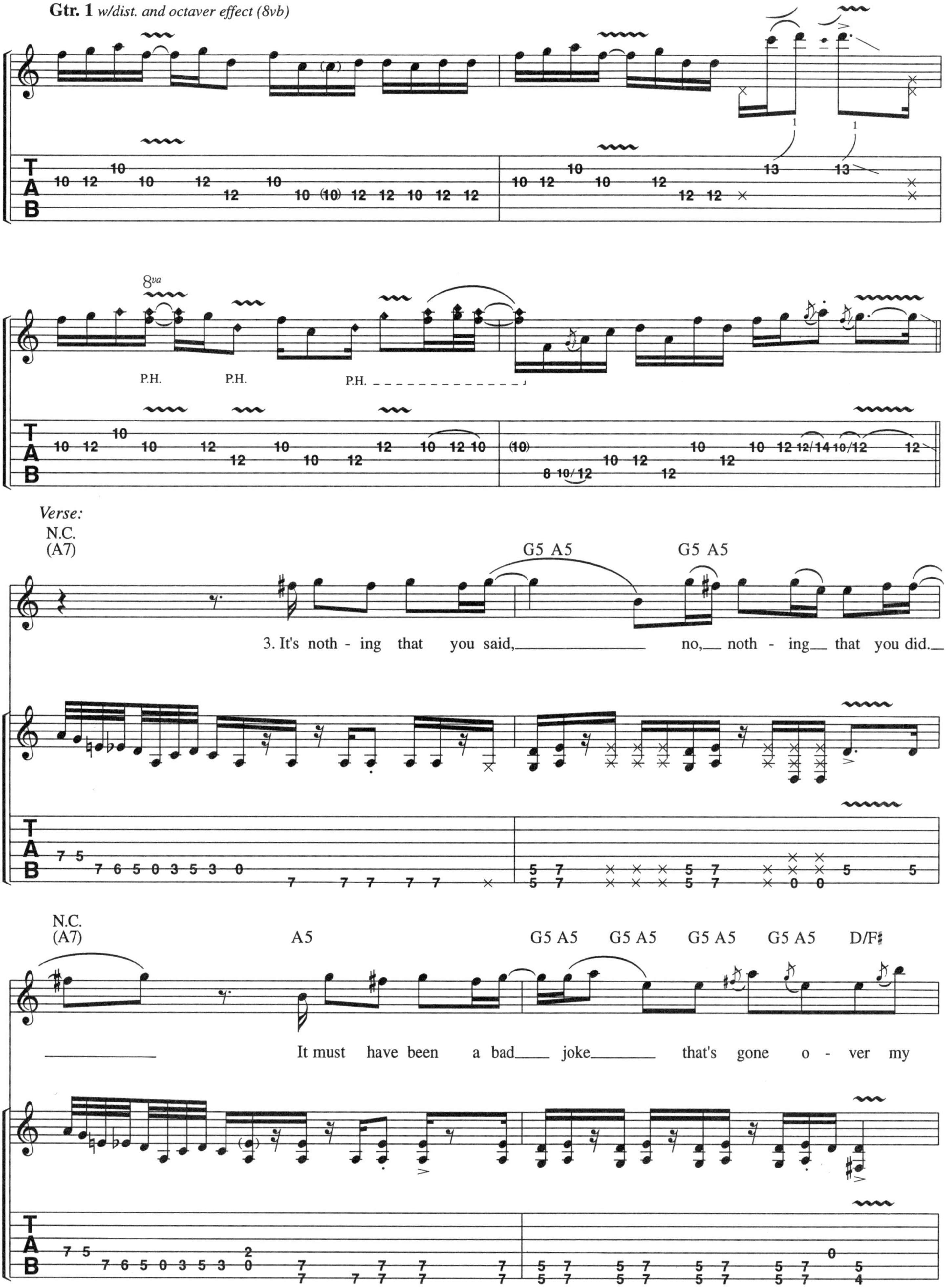
Gtr. 1 w/dist. and octaver effect (8vb)
8va
P.H.
P.H.
P.H.
Verse:
N.C.
(A7)
G5 A5
G5 A5
3. It's noth - ing that you said, no, noth - ing that you did.
N.C.
(A7)
A5
G5 A5
G5 A5
G5 A5
G5 A5
D/F♯
It must have been a bad joke that's gone o - ver my

head.___ What,___ me___ wor - ry___ an - oth - er trag - e - dy?___

The lat - ter plus time,___ e - quals com - e - dy.

Chorus:
w/Rhy. Fig. 1 *(Gtr. 1, 1st 3 bars) simile*

Why___ can't I___ get to the oth - er side,

I'm still___ wait - ing for the punch___ line.___ And

Gtr. 1

Waiting For The Punchline- 13 - 10
PG9515

who— ev- er said the grass al - ways grows— green- er on the oth - er, lied.—

I'm— still— wait- ing for the punch— line.—

Band tacet
Gtr. 1 *w/clean tone*

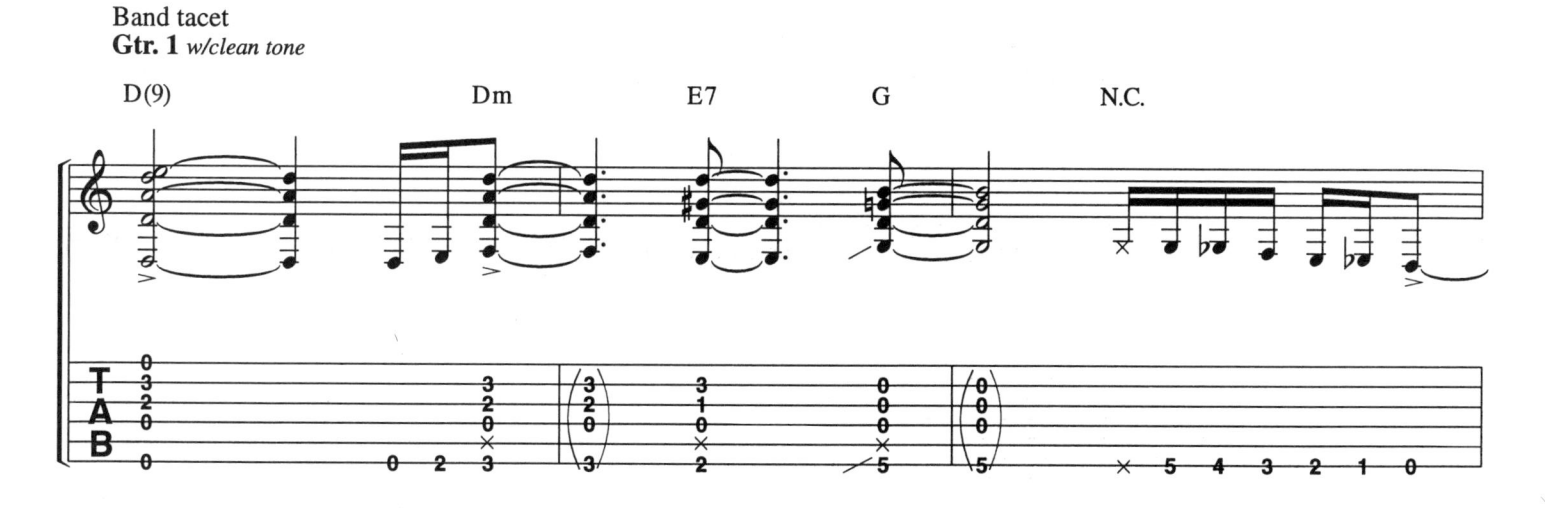

D(9)　　　　　Dm　　　E7　　G　　　N.C.

Waiting For The Punchline- 13 - 11
PG9515

Enter bass
D(9)
Dm
E7
G
D
let ring
Outro:
Dm
E7
G
N.C.
Yeah.
w/vcl. ad lib.
D(9)
Dm
E7
G
divisi
Rhy. Fig. 3
A
D5
Dm
E7
G

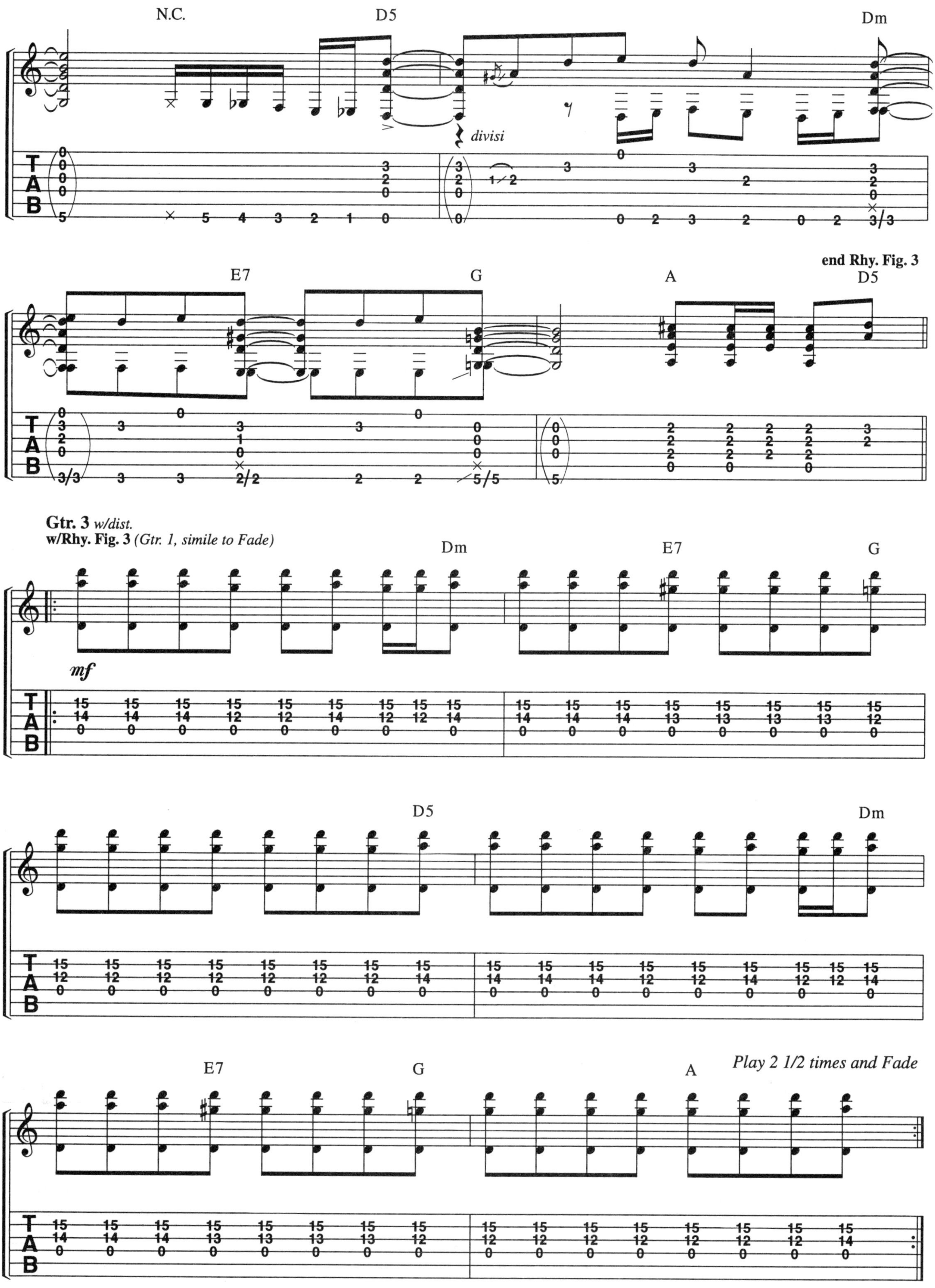

GUITAR TAB GLOSSARY **

TABLATURE EXPLANATION

READING TABLATURE: Tablature illustrates the six strings of the guitar. Notes and chords are indicated by the placement of fret numbers on a given string(s).

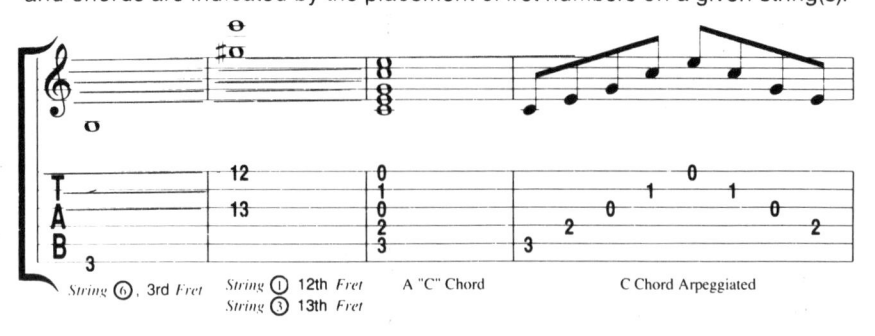

String ⑥, 3rd Fret   String ① 12th Fret   A "C" Chord   C Chord Arpeggiated
String ③ 13th Fret

BENDING NOTES

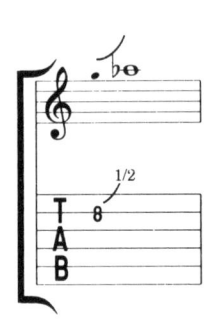

HALF STEP: Play the note and bend string one half step.*

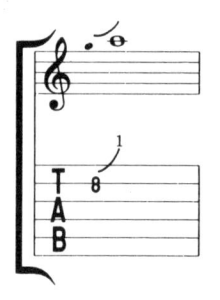

WHOLE STEP: Play the note and bend string one whole step.

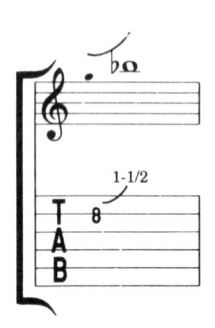

WHOLE STEP AND A HALF: Play the note and bend string a whole step and a half.

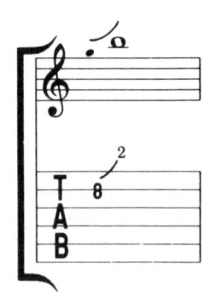

TWO STEPS: Play the note and bend string two whole steps.

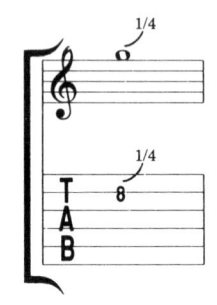

SLIGHT BEND (Microtone): Play the note and bend string slightly to the equivalent of half a fret.

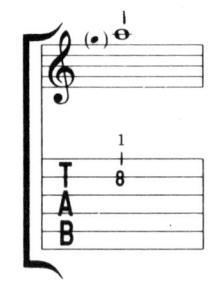

PREBEND (Ghost Bend): Bend to the specified note, before the string is picked.

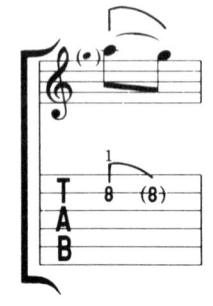

PREBEND AND RELEASE: Bend the string, play it, then release to the original note.

REVERSE BEND: Play the already-bent string, then immediately drop it down to the fretted note.

BEND AND RELEASE: Play the note and gradually bend to the next pitch, then release to the original note. Only the first note is attacked.

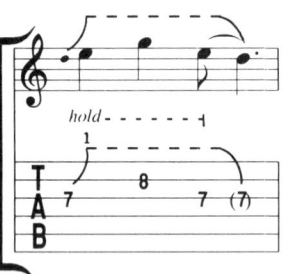

BENDS INVOLVING MORE THAN ONE STRING: Play the note and bend string while playing an additional note (or notes) on another string(s). Upon release, relieve pressure from additional note(s), causing original note to sound alone.

BENDS INVOLVING STATIONARY NOTES: Play notes and bend lower pitch, then hold until release begins (indicated at the point where line becomes solid).

UNISON BEND: Play both notes and immediately bend the lower note to the same pitch as the higher note.

DOUBLE NOTE BEND: Play both notes and immediately bend both strings simultaneously.

*A half step is the smallest interval in Western music; it is equal to one fret. A whole step equals two frets.

© 1990 Beam Me Up Music
c/o CPP/Belwin, Inc. Miami, Florida 33014
International Copyright Secured   Made in U.S.A.   All Rights Reserved

**By Kenn Chipkin and Aaron Stang

RHYTHM SLASHES

STRUM INDICATIONS: Strum with indicated rhythm. The chord voicings are found on the first page of the transcription underneath the song title.

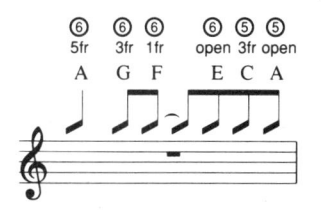

INDICATING SINGLE NOTES USING RHYTHM SLASHES: Very often single notes are incorporated into a rhythm part. The note name is indicated above the rhythm slash with a fret number and a string indication.

ARTICULATIONS

HAMMER ON: Play lower note, then "hammer on" to higher note with another finger. Only the first note is attacked.

LEFT HAND HAMMER: Hammer on the first note played on each string with the left hand.

PULL OFF: Play higher note, then "pull off" to lower note with another finger. Only the first note is attacked.

FRETBOARD TAPPING: "Tap" onto the note indicated by + with a finger of the pick hand, then pull off to the following note held by the fret hand.

TAP SLIDE: Same as fretboard tapping, but the tapped note is slid randomly up the fretboard, then pulled off to the following note.

BEND AND TAP TECHNIQUE: Play note and bend to specified interval. While holding bend, tap onto note indicated.

LEGATO SLIDE: Play note and slide to the following note. (Only first note is attacked).

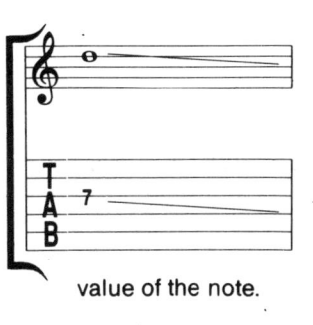

LONG GLISSANDO: Play note and slide in specified direction for the full value of the note.

SHORT GLISSANDO: Play note for its full value and slide in specified direction at the last possible moment.

PICK SLIDE: Slide the edge of the pick in specified direction across the length of the string(s).

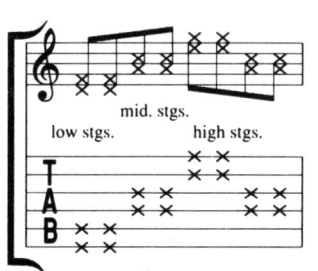

MUTED STRINGS: A percussive sound is made by laying the fret hand across all six strings while pick hand strikes specified area (low, mid, high strings).

PALM MUTE: The note or notes are muted by the palm of the pick hand by lightly touching the string(s) near the bridge.

TREMOLO PICKING: The note or notes are picked as fast as possible.

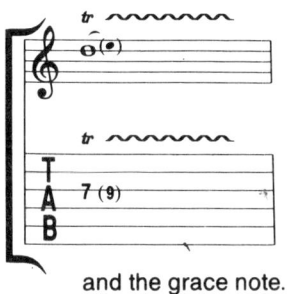

TRILL: Hammer on and pull off consecutively and as fast as possible between the original note and the grace note.

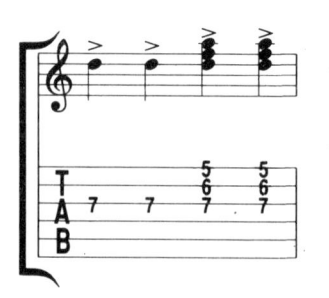

ACCENT: Notes or chords are to be played with added emphasis.

STACCATO (Detached Notes): Notes or chords are to be played roughly half their actual value and with separation.

DOWN STROKES AND UPSTROKES: Notes or chords are to be played with either a downstroke (⊓·) or upstroke (v) of the pick.

VIBRATO: The pitch of a note is varied by a rapid shaking of the fret hand finger, wrist, and forearm.

HARMONICS

NATURAL HARMONIC: A finger of the fret hand lightly touches the note or notes indicated in the tab and is played by the pick hand.

ARTIFICIAL HARMONIC: The first tab number is fretted, then the pick hand produces the harmonic by using a finger to lightly touch the same string at the second tab number (in parenthesis) and is then picked by another finger.

ARTIFICIAL "PINCH" HARMONIC: A note is fretted as indicated by the tab, then the pick hand produces the harmonic by squeezing the pick firmly while using the tip of the index finger in the pick attack. If parenthesis are found around the fretted note, it does not sound. No parenthesis means both the fretted note and A.H. are heard simultaneously.

TREMOLO BAR

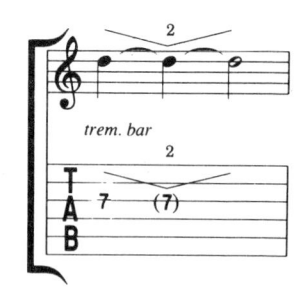

SPECIFIED INTERVAL: The pitch of a note or chord is lowered to a specified interval and then may or may not return to the original pitch. The activity of the tremolo bar is graphically represented by peaks and valleys.

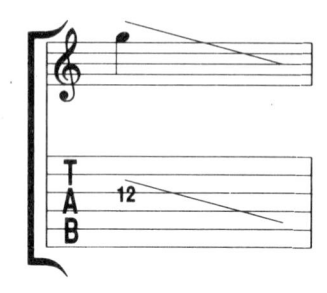

UN-SPECIFIED INTERVAL: The pitch of a note or a chord is lowered to an unspecified interval.